OUR LADY IN THE LITURGY

J. D. Crichton

Our Lady in the Liturgy

A Liturgical Press Book

THE LITURGICAL PRESS
Collegeville, Minnesota

This edition, 1997, published by
THE LITURGICAL PRESS
Collegeville, Minnesota 56321
in association with The Columba Press, Dublin, Ireland

Cover by Bill Bolger
The cover picture is a detail from *Holy Family with St John in a Landscape*
by Francesco Granacci and is used by permission of
The National Gallery of Ireland.
Origination by The Columba Press
Printed in Ireland by Colour Books Ltd, Dublin

Acknowledgements

Acknowledgement is made to A. P. Watt, Literary Agents for the
Liturgy Commission of England and Wales, for permission to quote ex-
tracts from patristic, later spiritual writers and single lines (antiphons)
from the Office of Readings and other offices as in the *Divine Office*
(Collins, Dwyer, Talbot, 1974). Bible quotations are from *The New
Jerusalem Bible* (Darton, Longman and Todd, London, 1985). Quotations
from the psalter are from *The Psalms* (Collins, London, 1963). For the
Constitution on the Church, see *Vatican II: Conciliar and Post Conciliar
Documents*, revised ed. 1988, Austin Flannery OP (Dominican Public-
ations, Dublin).

Library of Congress Cataloging-in-Publication Data
Crichton, J. D. (James Dunlop), 1907–
    Our Lady in the Liturgy / J. D. Crichton
        p. cm.
    Includes bibliographical references
    ISBN 0-8146-2493-6
    1. Mary, Blessed Virgin, Saint, in the liturgy – Catholic Church.
2. Catholic Church – Liturgy. I. Title
BT645.3.C75 1997
232.91 – dc21   97–13583
                                                                        CIP

Contents

Preface   7

1.   The Blessed Virgin Mary,
     the Mystery of Christ and the church   9

2.   The First Feast of Mary   23

3.   Mary the Mother of God   27

4.   The Presentation of the Lord   34

5.   The Annunciation of the Lord   40

6.   The Visitation of the Blessed Virgin Mary   47

7.   The Assumption of the Blessed Virgin Mary   52

8.   The Nativity of the Blessed Virgin Mary   60

9.   The Immaculate Conception of the
     Blessed Virgin Mary   64

10. The Blessed Virgin Mary in Advent   69

11. Our Lady of Sorrows   76

12. The Presentation of the Blessed Virgin Mary   81

13. Other Celebrations of the Blessed Virgin Mary   83

14. Some Marian Chants   94

15. The Psalms in the Marian Feasts   103

Preface

Books of devotion about the Blessed Virgin Mary are probably countless. This is not one of them, though the author hopes that what is written here may lead to reflection and so to prayer. This book is an exploration of the feasts of the Blessed Virgin and their meaning. The origins of the greater feasts of Mary are to be found long ago in the fifth century in the eastern part of the great church that was still undivided. With one exception, the churches of the east and west still celebrate those feasts. As I have indicated in various places of the book, the contribution of the eastern churches to Marian liturgy is very considerable. In my commentaries I have tried to keep close to the great tradition, that is to the place and role of Mary in the history of salvation – a point insisted upon by the Second Vatican Council in its *Constitution on the Church* and especially in chapter 8 – and to the close and indeed intimate association of the Virgin Mother to her Son, Jesus Christ. As Pope Paul VI in his *Marialis Cultus* remarked, 'Certain practices of piety that not long ago seemed suitable for expressing the religious sentiments of individuals and Christian communities, seem today inadequate or unsuitable because they are linked with social and cultural patterns of the past.' He sought to restore a balance of which he gives an example: 'The Advent liturgy, by linking the awaiting of the Messiah and the awaiting of the glorious return of Christ with the admirable commemoration of his mother, presents a happy balance in worship. This balance can be taken as a norm for preventing any tendency (as has happened at times in certain forms of popular piety) to separate devotion to the Blessed Virgin from its necessary point of reference – Christ' (para 4). This was but to restate the older tradition of both the east and the west. In the art tradition of the west, from the Middle Ages onwards, Mary is always visibly associated with Jesus. It is this tradition that underlies the study of the Marian feasts in this book.

Yet there have been other developments. From about the twelfth century, there has been a concentration on the Blessed Virgin herself and this has found expression in what are called the minor feasts of Mary, which I have considered in a separate chapter.

In addition, it seemed right to include a chapter on some of the Marian chants and prayers which in fact form part of the liturgy. Some of them, even the familiar Hail Mary (in its present form), have a somewhat complicated history. Finally, the use of the psalms, a matter of some difficulty, as used in the Divine Office, seemed to call for consideration and I have attempted an interpretation. Further work on this matter seems to be called for and I leave that to the experts in holy scripture.

CHAPTER 1

The Blessed Virgin Mary,
the Mystery of Christ and the church

This, with the inclusion of 'Mother of God', is the title of the chapter (8) attached to the *Constitution on the Church* of the Second Vatican Council. It was something of a watershed in the matter of the liturgical practice and devotion concerning Mary, the Mother of God. It is not too much to say that, in some quarters, devotion had become a little over-heated. Titles like Mediatrix and Co-Redemptrix were in circulation, sometimes without the necessary precautions. The council was concerned to place the Blessed Virgin Mary in the plan of salvation (*oikonomia*: God's arrangement; the word is difficult to translate) for the human race. Accordingly, the council evoked the story of Genesis 3:15. The seed of the woman would vanquish the serpent, the symbol of evil, thus giving the promise of eventual redemption. Likewise, the prophecy of Isaiah 7:14 is recalled, about the maiden who will bear a son whose name will be Emmanuel. In the words of the Constitution, 'After a long period of waiting, the times are fulfilled in her, the exalted daughter of Zion, and the plan of salvation is established when the Son of God has taken human nature from her, that he might in the mysteries of his flesh free man from sin' (*Constitution*, no. 55). If we turn to the infancy gospel of Luke we find that it is concerned with salvation from beginning to end. At the circumcision of John the Baptist there is the classical blessing prayer (the *Benedictus*) heralding the salvation of the human race, a salvation of which John will be the forerunner:

> 'Blessed be the Lord God of Israel,
> for he has visited his people, he has come to rescue them (to redeem them).
> He has raised up for us a *power of salvation*,'
> a salvation proclaimed by the prophets throughout the ages,
> that he would '*save* us from our enemies', ...

showing mercy to the ancestors, he remembers his holy
covenant that the people would be his and he would be their
God. The child will be a prophet, he will go before the Lord to
prepare the way for him, and the people, coming to the knowledge of the salvation that awaits them, will be saved from their
sins through the tender mercy of God.

Luke 1:24-38 can be seen as a climax of salvation history which is
recalled in several ways. To the 'Son of the Most High' will be
given the throne of his ancestor David and he will rule over the
house of Jacob for ever, but the house will become the family of
God, the new people of God who will be members of Christ,
forming with him the One Body. For Mary herself the coming of
the one who would be her son was the culmination and fulfilment of God's promises made to Israel: 'My soul proclaims the
greatness of the Lord, and my spirit exults in God my *Saviour.*'
The Almighty has done great things for her and his mercy reaches
from age to age, from one generation to another right up to this
moment when she is declared the Mother of God (verse 35). But
this divine mercy is the same that was shown to 'Abraham and
to his descendants' as it will be for ever through her Son, Jesus,
Saviour (verse 31). Indeed, the appointed time, the *kairos*, had
come, 'God sent his son, born of a woman, born subject of the
law, to *redeem* the subjects of the law and to enable us to be
adopted as sons' by the grace of the Redeemer (Gal 4:4, 5).

We find the same message in other parts of the infancy gospel.
At the birth of Jesus he is proclaimed Saviour: 'Today in the
town of *David* a *Saviour* is born to you' (2:11) and the whole of
creation cries out, 'Glory to God in the highest heaven and peace
(reconciliation) to those who enjoy his (God's) favour'. Then the
Redeemer was brought to be 'redeemed' in the Temple (2:22-34)
and Simeon, an upright and devout man who was looking forward to Israel's comforting, took 'salvation' in his arms and proclaimed, 'My eyes have seen the salvation (*sotérion*) which you
have prepared all nations to see, a light to enlighten the pagans
and the glory of your people Israel'. But prophetically he was
aware that Mary had a part to play in that salvation: many
would rise and fall in Israel, her son was a sign of contradiction,
and a sword of sorrow and suffering would pierce her soul. In

the mind of Simeon (and Luke), Mary would be associated with the suffering of her son.

Luke too, taking up a theme of the last years of the Old Testament, brings on to the stage the prophetess Anna who, with Mary and Joseph, with Zechariah and Elizabeth, with Simeon himself and no doubt others, are the 'poor ones', the *anawim*, the humble who were open to God's message and who were awaiting 'the deliverance of Israel'. They too belonged to Israel, they were looking for a Messiah and now he was in their midst. Yet they did not realise fully who or what this child was. When Jesus reached maturity ('he was twelve years old') he was found in the Temple, where he had been offered, among the 'doctors, listening and asking them questions' (2:46). Neither Mary nor Joseph understood (2:29) that Jesus might begin to be 'busy with my Father's affairs'. It was perhaps the first of the sorrows of Mary. As St Luke also suggests, it was the beginning of the work of salvation.[1] The role of Mary is thus made clear in salvation history which continues and is brought to its climax in the life, passion, death and resurrection of her son. She is at the beginning of the saving work of Jesus and she is with him at the end when Jesus hands her over to the beloved disciple, a symbol (though a real person) of the Christian community, the church, where Mary is present as she and the other women and disciples pray for the coming of the Holy Spirit (Acts 1:14).

It is clear, then, that Mary's role in salvation history was not passive. She gave of her self and her own body to the formation of that human nature which the Son of God took up 'for us and for our salvation'. This she did by the total giving of herself to God's saving purpose when she said, 'Let it be done to me according to your word'. She aligned her own will with the will of God though she did not know where this would lead her or what it would lead to. This self-giving, which after all is the supreme expression of love, endured throughout her life, through the doubts and misunderstandings of Jesus' public ministry to the pain she experienced as she saw her son in agony on the cross. Her 'ministry' to the ministry of her son is summed up this way in chapter 8 of the *Constitution on the Church* (no. 56):

'Behold the handmaid of the Lord, be it done to me according
to thy word' (Lk 1:38). Thus the daughter of Adam, Mary,
consenting to the word of God, became the Mother of Jesus.
Committing herself whole-heartedly and impeded by no sin
to God's saving will, she devoted herself totally, as a handmaid of the Lord, to the person and work of her son, under
and with him, serving the mystery of redemption, by the
grace of almighty God. Rightly therefore, the Fathers (of the
church) see Mary not merely as passively engaged by God,
but freely co-operating in the work of man's salvation
through faith and obedience. For, as St Irenaeus says, she
'being obedient, became the cause of salvation for herself and
for the whole human race'.[2]

The text then speaks of the 'union of the mother and the son in
the work of salvation' and sees this union as manifested in
Christ's life and ministry, though it does not define the word
'union'. Much has been written about the knowledge of Mary or,
more precisely, her understanding of the nature and mission of
her son, but the evidence is conflicting. In Luke 1 he is declared
'the Son of the Most High' yet, in Luke 2, she does not understand why he has left her and Joseph and is about his Father's affairs in the Temple. This caused her sorrow and anxiety (2:48,
50). What she felt when he left home when he 'was about thirty
years old' is not recorded but during his ministry there occurred
the incidents recorded in John 2:1-11 and Mark 3:31-35. At the
marriage feast of Cana she did not understand the meaning of
the 'hour': 'My hour has not yet come', the 'hour' when he
would begin his mission, when he would proclaim the coming
of the kingdom. This would be accompanied by miracles, and
his ministry would come to a conclusion in the hour when he
would die on a cross.

Then there is the event that seems to have troubled the other
evangelists. In the midst of his ministry, when he and his disciples were besieged by the crowds so that they had no time even
to eat and his relatives thought he was out of his mind (Mk 3:20,
21), his mother and brothers arrived, evidently greatly concerned for him. They asked to see him but their request is not
granted. Instead Jesus says, 'Who are my mother and brothers?'

The saying is not without its difficulties, but it will be helpful to
take the whole passage in which it occurs, 3:20-35. It might seem,
at first sight, that the relatives thought Jesus was overdoing it.
They had observed or been told that he had said extraordinary
things and that he had worked miracles. In short, they did not
understand what his mission was or what sort of mission he had
committed himself to. But the statement 'he is out of his mind'
had a more sinister meaning than might appear. As the next passage, 22-27, shows, being out of one's mind suggested demonic
possession and this was precisely the allegation made by the
'scribes from Jerusalem'. Jesus refutes this and then it is that his
mother and brothers come and join the crowd where he is. They
ask to see him, perhaps with the intention of taking him home.
Then comes Jesus' question, 'Who are my mother and brothers?'
Answering his own question and looking at the disciples
around him he says, 'Here are my mother and brothers'. Then
comes the key statement: 'Whoever does the will of God is my
brother and sister and mother.' This seems to echo the saying we
find in Matthew 7:21, 'It is not those who *say* to me, "Lord, Lord"
who will enter the kingdom of heaven'. We can refer to Luke
1:38 also: 'Be it done to me according to your word' and to his account of the Markan incident where he writes: 'My mother and
brother are those who hear the *word* of God and put it into practice' (8:21).

In any case, it seems to be one of those sayings of Jesus that emphasises that 'the ties of physical relationship yield to those of
spiritual relationship' (see *NJB*, Mt 12:46-50, note q). Jesus was
actively engaged in his mission and nothing must interfere with
it. We may conclude that Mary may not have understood the nature of her son's mission or did not fully understand it. But she
had given her consent to the will of God long before and, like
other human beings who try and do likewise, she did not see all
the consequences of her original act of faith and trust in God.
Though this is the only instance in the synoptic gospels of
Mary's presence during his ministry, it is an indication that her
acceptance of God's will endure throughout her life. This is the
view of the council document (no. 62): Mary continued to give
her consent until the cross.

Mary was with her son at the end of his life (Jn 19:25-27). That she suffered with her son is beyond doubt, but was she doing more? The council document sees in her presence a co-operation with her son in his self-offering: 'No creature could ever be classed with the Incarnate Word and Redeemer. But, just as the priesthood of Christ is shared in various ways both by sacred ministers and by the faithful, and as the one goodness of God is in reality communicated diversely to his creatures, so also the unique mediation of the Redeemer does not exclude, but rather gives rise to, manifold co-operation which is but a sharing in this unique source'.

> 'The church does not hesitate to profess this subordination of the role of Mary. She (the church) experiences it continuously and commends it to the hearts of the faithful, so that encouraged by this maternal help they may more closely adhere to the Mediator and Redeemer' (no. 62).[3]

Thus we can say that Mary was with her son, associated with his redeeming work from the beginning to the end of his earthly life. But salvation history continues in the messianic era when indeed the covenantal relationship of the people of God is brought to perfection and to an intimacy unimaginable in the Old Testament. In this new order Mary has a special role to play. 'By reason of the gift and role of her divine motherhood, by which she is united with her son, the Redeemer, and with her unique graces and functions, the Blessed Virgin is also *intimately united to the church*. As St Ambrose taught (*Expos in Luc*. II, PL 15, L555), the mother of God is a type of the church in the order of faith, charity and perfect union with Christ. For in the mystery of the church, which is rightly called mother and virgin, the Blessed Virgin stands out in eminent and singular fashion as both virgin and mother' (*Constitution on the Church*, no. 63). Mary has a special relationship to the church which can be traced in the scriptures, notably in the Johannine writings, the fourth gospel and Revelation. In the gospel, Mary is addressed as 'woman' both in 2:4 and in 19:26, and in Revelation 12:1. All these sayings are in the context of salvation: in John 2 Jesus' 'hour' has not yet come, the hour of his redeeming work; in John 19 Jesus, hanging on the cross, gives John to his mother; in

Revelation we have the mysterious figure of the woman who brings forth a child that is persecuted by Satan. This in turn recalls the woman in Genesis 3:15 who will be involved in the struggle between good and evil. This text too is the first adumbration of the salvation of the human race by the 'seed' of the woman. It seems to be agreed that Revelation 12 refers to the church. The woman brings forth the child in pain and anguish, Satan attacks, the child is swept up to be with God (the resurrection and ascension), and the woman flees into the wilderness symbolising the time of the church, the old and the new Israel (for the new is in continuation with the old) is brought to birth through suffering and tribulation comparable to the pains of childbirth (cf. Jn 16:21-22 and for the Old Testament see Is 26:17-18, 66:7). But many commentators are agreed that here there is a secondary symbol, that of Mary who brings forth the child 'who is to rule the nations with a rod of iron', a reference to the messianic psalm, 2:9 (cf. also psalm 109[110]) which in the Christian tradition has always been interpreted as speaking of the Messiah. What the text suggests is that the mother of 12:1 is also the mother of Jesus who will accompany the church throughout the future and will care for it. We are coming close to the notion of Mary as the Mother of the Church. This secondary symbolism can be seen in John 2:1-11 where the new wine is a symbol of the new, rich and abundant order, the messianic age to which the church is central. Mary has a care for that church of the new covenant. Likewise in John 19:26, 27, Mary is made the (adoptive) mother of the Christian community represented by the beloved disciple.[4]

We can take this a step further from a different point of view. Paul VI gave Mary the title 'Mother of the Church'. Is this a mere metaphor, on the one hand saying too little, or on the other suggesting too much? It is a case of analogy, of likenesses and unlikenesses of Mary to the church. Mary in faith and obedience conceived and brought forth Christ 'overshadowed by the Holy Spirit'. The church 'by preaching and by baptism brings forth to a new and immortal life children who are conceived by the power of the Holy Spirit and born of God'. This is supported by a quotation from a Christmas sermon of Leo the Great's: 'The origin which (Christ) took in the womb of the virgin he has given to the baptismal font: he has given to water what he had given to his mother; the power of the Most High and the over-shadowing of the Holy Spirit which was responsible for Mary's bringing forth the Saviour, had the same effect, so that water may regenerate the believer' (Tract. 25, *Marialis Cultus*, no. 19). More succinctly the Spanish or Mozarabic Liturgy has the phrase, 'Mary carried life in her womb; the church bears life in the waters of baptism' (*M.C. ibid*). Christians are the adopted children of Christ and through the relationship with him, formed in baptism, we become children of Mary also. It is a rela-tionship based on and brought about by the grace of Jesus Christ.

Thus related to her, it is for us to look to her as a model or an ex-ample for our own life. This can be seen in several ways as set out both in chapter 8 of the *Constitution on the Church* and in the *Marialis Cultus* of Paul VI. But first a word or two much be said about the word 'model'. On the whole, people do not like 'model' personages, those who are 'perfect' and never do any-thing wrong. Various images and writings about Mary come close to suggesting that sort of thing. It needs to be said, then, that Mary was 'an entirely human person'.[5] She was a girl of the village of Nazareth, she went daily to draw water from the well, she had to do all the housework and in addition probably had to make clothes for her husband and Jesus. She had the same feel-ings as other people, she walked through the dusty hill-country to be with Elizabeth and for at least a time she seems to have fol-lowed Jesus in his missionary journeys. We can only speculate what she felt when Jesus left home, but from the gospels we know that she suffered with her son as he lay in agony on the cross. Whatever and however many exalted titles are give to her, she remains a fully human being, closer than anyone else to her son, Jesus, but gloriously human.

Once that is understood we can go on to consider how Mary is a model or an example for human beings. Some of these are set out in the *Marialis Cultus* where the Pope was concerned to show how feasts of the liturgy and certain devotions keep Mary's virtues before the minds of those who celebrate and use them.

The first to be singled out is faith. The message came to her and in St Luke's account it came near to overwhelming her. She was troubled and indeed greatly troubled, one could say she was shaken. But however much or little she understood of the sublime vocation to which she was being called, she gave her consent, she believed and for her faith she was blessed: 'Blessed is she who believed that the promise made her by the Lord would be fulfilled' (Lk 1:45). This faith endured. She believed in her son when she asked him to save the wedding couple from embarrassment by providing some more wine. She believed when she stood at the foot of the cross and heard her son call her 'mother'. Her faith, however, was an all-embracing faith, not just an 'intellectual' faith. She gave her whole self to the work of God, 'Be it done to me according to your word'.

This faith was born of her attentiveness to the word. After the birth of Jesus, after all that had happened, after the visit of the shepherds, she treasured all these things and 'pondered them in her heart' (and cf. Lk 2:51). She was attentive to the word but that word became event; the shepherds went to 'see this *thing* (*réma*) that had happened' and she reflected on the great event of the birth of Jesus revealed by the *réma* the angel had spoken to her and to which she had given her free consent: 'Be it done to me according to your *word*'. Filled with love – for there was no obstacle in her heart – she responded readily and generously to the word of God that came to her, and as St Augustine and St Leo said, *prius concepit mente quam corpore* (she conceived the word first in her heart and then in her body). The message for ourselves is clear.

The doing of God's will is at the centre of the Christian life and Mary more than anyone was a model and exemplar of acceptance of the will of God for her own life and vocation. This is clear from the whole story of the annunciation, from her going to the Temple with Joseph to offer Jesus and to do all that was *according to the law* (Lk 2:22), to the acceptance of her destiny which was obscurely foreshadowed by Simeon: 'A sword will pierce your own soul too', as the lance on Calvary would pierce the heart of her son.

The doing of God's will is often fraught with uncertainty: what is God's will for me in these circumstances and at this time? Whatever Mary understood of what great things the Almighty had done for her and in her, she did not know the consequences, she did not know what the joys or the sorrows her doing God's will would bring upon her. Yet she accepted, she was the 'lowly handmaid', the *doulé*, the 'slave' of the Lord, and she praised the name of the Lord for all this (Lk 1:48, 49). But Mary's acceptance of God's will was not simply passive or submissive. She actively embraced it: 'I am the handmaid of the Lord; be it done to me according to your word', and again and more forcefully, 'My soul (my whole being) proclaims the greatness of the Lord and my spirit exults in God my saviour, because he has looked upon his lowly handmaid ...'. She embraced God's will with immense love and so became the perfect follower among the Christian people of her own son: 'It is not those who say to me "Lord, Lord" who will enter the kingdom of heaven but the person who does the will of my father in heaven' (Mt 7:21).

Then there is that different virtue, humility, which for St Benedict was the foundation of the spiritual life. But Mary's humility was not of the unreal, cringing sort. Like a good Jewess she was aware of the majesty of God, she was aware of her littleness before him, she was a village girl and unmarried, of no account to anyone. But she was strong and, if the hymn of the Magnificat expresses her sentiments (as we may suppose), she realised the almightiness of God and her own lowly state. How could it be that such a one as she could be called to a mysterious and high vocation? But because God called her she accepted, in spite of everything that might come. Humility is the virtue of the strong, not of the weak. She seems to have practised this virtue throughout her life, for if Jesus' life for some thirty years was a hidden life so was hers. Only once does she appear in his public life (Mk 3:31-35) when perhaps she was anxious for her son. (The Cana incident was just *before* the beginning of Jesus' public ministry.) She appears in public at the end to be with him and to suffer with him. The last we hear of her is with the apostles, in prayer (Acts 1:14). The New Testament does not tell us a great deal about Mary but we get the impression that she was the still centre of the sublime events in which she was involved. On Christmas night she utters not a word; all we are told is that she treasured all that had been said and done and pondered it in her heart. On Calvary she was silent, hearing and accepting the last words her son addressed to her and the beloved disciple. With the apostles she prayed, awaiting the coming of the Holy Spirit, that Spirit who had come to her so many years before and who would renew divine grace within her so that she could become the mother of the church. Her prayer seems to have been fundamentally contemplative (Lk 2:19 and 51) and perhaps that is why she seems to be the still centre of all that was happening around her.

Even if, however, commentators nowadays hold that Mary was not the author of the Magnificat, we may, I think, assume that at least the first part of it expresses her sentiments (the middle part certainly expresses Lukan views) and if so, then we see that her prayer was theocentric. Like any devout Jew she blessed, praised, thanked God, the Almighty, for the great things he had done for her. His name, he himself, was holy, and his mercy, his faithful love, extends through the generations of those who revere him as she did. Here we find humility combined with trust; she is the lowly handmaid who, contemplating the greatness of God and the faithful love of God, can rejoice and exult in the God who brings salvation to her and to all the descendants of her race and, we may say, of the new race of Christians brought into existence by her son. With this is connected her prayer for us which from very early times (the third century) the church has believed she makes. It is usually called 'intercession' but this word sometimes gives trouble to some non-Catholic Christians. Chapter 8 of the *Constitution on the Church* puts this matter in its true perspective:

> In the words of the apostle there is but one mediator: "for there is but one God and one mediator of God and men, the man Jesus Christ, who gave himself a redemption for all" (1 Tim 2:5, 6). But Mary's function as mother of men in no way diminishes this unique mediation of Christ, but rather shows its power. But the Blessed Virgin's salutary influence on men originates not in any inner necessity but in the disposition of

God. It flows forth from the superabundance of the merits of Christ, *rests on his mediation, depends entirely on it* and *draws all its power from it*. It does not hinder in any way the immediate union of the faithful with Christ but, on the contrary, fosters it' (no. 60, italics mine).

Mary, the sinless one, the first and chief of the redeemed, is nearest to her son. There was not and is not any barrier between herself and him, and with her deep faith and trust she can enfold her intercession in his 'who is ever living to make intercession for us' (Heb 7:25).

With her intercession for us she brings her love for us, but more particularly her love for her son. That her love for him was unparalleled can hardly be doubted. She gave herself to God's will and purpose with the total commitment of mind and heart. She conceived Jesus in her mind before she conceived him in her body. The body and mind and heart of Jesus was formed in and from her body. She was nearer to him than any other human being that has ever existed, and in her care for him in infancy and childhood she expressed her love even if we have no details of those hidden years. She stood at the foot of the cross but we can only guess the anguished love that filled her soul. Indeed, if it was a hidden love it was undoubtedly a great love, a greater love than anyone before or since has had for Jesus. This is well expressed in the second Advent Preface: 'His future coming was proclaimed by the prophets. The virgin mother bore him in her womb with love beyond all telling.'

Such then is the image of the Blessed Virgin Mary that is presented to us by the Second Vatican Council. It is noble, it is appealing, and we may see it as the crowning of the work of another council, that of Ephesus in 431, which declared that Mary is *Theotokos*, the God-bearer, the mother of Jesus who is the Son of God.

Notes

1. The 'factuality' of the infancy gospels is not a question into which I wish to go here. It seems to me however that the infancy gospels of Matthew and Luke represent certain traditions that were current in the first century AD. But the tradition, or sometimes the traditions, have often been spoken of as *un*written. Here in Matthew and Luke we have *written* traditions. Luke indeed says that he has investigated the traditions exactly or accurately ('accounts of the events that have taken place among us, exactly as they were handed down'). He has carefully gone over the whole story from the beginning (1:1-3). St Paul also speaks of what has been *'handed down'* (1 Cor 11:23-26 and 15:3) on two crucial matters of the Christian faith, the eucharist and the resurrection of Christ. This, as in Matthew and Luke (cf. 2:10), was the proclamation of the good news of salvation which was reflected on by the early Christian communities and then written down. In that process there was development. Both Matthew and Luke saw very clearly that Jesus was the promised Messiah, the Saviour, the Son of God. That is the main burden of their accounts and that is what is of supreme import-ance, as those same accounts make clear. The details of the narratives fall in second place behind that great theological statement.

2. *'Cause* of salvation'. This seems rather strong. Irenaeus's works sur-vive in a Latin translation (except for some fragments in Greek) and the word is *principium* which I presume in the Greek was *arché* which means 'beginning' (see Jn 1:1), 'source', 'origin' (see Lampe, s.v, *arché, Greek Patristic Lexicon*, OUP, 1961/1978). *Principium* can also be translated 'beginning' rather than 'cause' and that would seem to be its sense here. Mary conceived by the Holy Spirit and brought forth Jesus Christ the Son of God and so 'began' the salvation of the human race. In so far as she bore Jesus in her womb she could be said to be the 'origin' of salva-tion. In Thomistic terms she could be said to be an *instrumental* cause though not an inert one. She gave her consent, 'Be it done to me…'.

3. Trans. from *The Documents of Vatican II*, ed. Walter M. Abbott SJ and Joseph Gallagher (London-Dublin, 1966), p. 92, which is closer to the original than that in Flannery, *Vatcian II*, vol. 1, p. 419. The statement is made in the context of certain titles that at one time or another have been given to Mary: Advocate, Helper, Benefactress and Mediatrix. These however must be correctly understood so that they do not take away or add anything to the dignity and efficacy of Christ the one Redeemer (no. 62). 'Co-redemptress' is not included in the list yet it and 'Mediatrix' are the most contentious and, in my view, the most likely to lead people astray. It would seem better that they should not be used at all.

4. For all this matter see R. E. Brown, *The Gospel according to John* (Geoffrey Chapman, London, 1984); for John 1:11, vol. 1, pp. 108-9 and for John 19:26, 27, vol. II, pp. 992-925. The author is duly cautious, care-ful not to read too much into the texts.

5 For a further development of this see John Macquarrie, *Mary for All Christians* (London, 1990), p. 24. Cf. also pp. 25-6: 'The title (Mother of God) is highly exalted because it puts in the strongest possible language the indispensable part which Mary played *as a human being and a woman*, in the economy of salvation. If there was to be an incarnation, then there had to be a woman as the necessary agent. And obviously, it could not be any woman, as if all that mattered was conceiving and bearing a child. It had to be a woman singularly 'graced' or 'favoured' of God (Lk 1:28 and 30)'. (Italics mine.)

CHAPTER 2

The First Feast of Mary

It may surprise some that there was no Marian feast in the first four centuries of the church. In the first century the only celebration or feast was the Lord's Day or Sunday (cf. Apoc 1:10), observed every week, and in the second that of the Paschal Mystery of the Lord's passion, death and resurrection celebrated once a year at what we call Easter time. There is, however, another way of looking at things. The infancy gospels of Matthew and Luke are in their own way celebrations of Mary, the Mother of God. She is the mother 'of the son of the Most High' of whose kingdom there will never be an end (Lk 1:32, 33); she is the mother of Emmanuel who is God-with-us (Mt 1:23). She is both virgin (Lk 1:34) and mother (Lk 1:43, 44), and when she gives birth to Jesus, the Son of God, the heavens as it were opened and a voice proclaims that the child is the saviour 'who is Christ the Lord' (Lk 1:11). The solemnity of these narratives and their theological density are impressive and they seem to have been written down (among other reasons) to honour Mary, the virgin-mother of Nazareth.

Apart from this 'celebration' it would be some long time before there was a feast of Mary. Like theology, liturgy takes time to develop, and the church, reflecting on the data of revelation, gradually comes to a deeper understanding of it and of the role of the Blessed Virgin Mary in salvation history. This begins to be apparent from the middle of the second century when St Justin the Martyr contrasts Eve in her disobedience with Mary in her obedience to the word of God. The same teaching, more elaborated, is found in Irenaeus who wrote: 'Eve by her disobedience brought death upon herself and all the human race; Mary by her obedience brought salvation' (*Adv. Haer.* III, xxii, 4). The term *Theotokos*

(Mary) who gave birth to the Son of God, was used by Origen about 250. The Council of Ephesus, which met in 431, was, however, both a watershed and a catalyst. It defined as a doctrine of faith that Mary is *Theotokos* which was translated into Latin as *(Maria), Dei Genetrix* (Mother of God) or, it seems more accurately, *Deipara*, God-bearer. This definition also stimulated devotion to Mary and celebrations in her honour in the liturgy. It was after Ephesus that feasts of our Lady began to be instituted. The oldest Marian feasts are found in the Holy Land where memories of Mary still remained. According to legend, appearing as early as the middle of the second century, Mary, on her way to Bethlehem to give birth to Jesus, rested at a certain place before going further. Here, in the early fifth century, a chapel or sanctuary was built by a lady called Ikelia and a feast called the *Kathisma* (literally the sitting-down-place) was kept. Later it was transferred to Jerusalem where the reputed tomb of Mary was venerated in Gethsemane. At first it seems to have been a feast of Mary Theotokos and then it became the feast of her Dormition or *Anapausis*, the Falling Asleep. This took place about 450. Thus the oldest feast of Mary had its origin in the eastern church. It combined her motherhood with her Dormition which, in the west, came to be called her Assumption. In the sixth century the Emperor Justinian ordered the celebration of the feast throughout the empire.[1]

The feast made its way to the west where in Rome in the seventh century popes of eastern origin reigned. It is recorded in the *Liber Pontificalis* as the Dormition, in a gospel book as the *Pausatio*, and a century later, in the *Sacramentary* of Pope Hadrian, it was called the Assumption of the Blessed Virgin Mary.

There was a grand celebration. A procession from the Lateran when an icon of Christ (of Byzantine provenance) called the *Sacratisima imago Domini Dei et Salvatoris nostri acheropsita (sic) nuncupatur* (The sacred image of our Lord God and our Saviour Jesus Christ, not made by hands, as it is called) was carried amidst much incense and the singing of a chant, the text of which survives, to the church of St Mary Major.[2] There on arrival it was 'greeted' by another icon, one of Mary, called *Salus populi Romani* (the salvation – well being? – of the Roman peo-

ple). The two icons were set up together and then the pope celebrated the Mass of the Assumption. It was in this same century
that the four feasts of the Annunciation to Mary, the
Presentation of the Lord in the Temple (both fundamentally
feasts of the Lord), the Assumption and the Nativity of the
Blessed Virgin Mary, appear in the official documents of the
time. In the *Liber Pontificalis* we read that Pope Sergius (of Syrian
origin) added to the celebration of these feasts four solemn pro-
cessions, no doubt of the kind attached to the celebration of the
Assumption. To these must be added the feast of Mary on 1
January which has been called 'the first Marian feast of the
Roman liturgy'.[3] All this does not mean that there was no vener-
ation of Mary in Rome or the west until this time. In the Roman
Canon of the Mass we have the phrase: '(Making the memory of)
gloriosae semper Virginis Mariae Genetricis *Dei et Domini Nostri* (of
the glorious Virgin Mary, *Mother of God*, our Lord Jesus Christ).
It is thought with some plausibility that Pope Xystus III inserted
these words into the Canon when he dedicated the church of St
Mary Major in 432, a year after the closing of the Council of
Ephesus. Then, as has been said above, there is what is said to be
the unique Roman feast of Mary, that was celebrated in the
church of *Sancta Maria ad Martyres*, the old Roman Pantheon
which was dedicated as a church in the early seventh century.
For many centuries the feast was somewhat obscured by the in-
troduction of the feast of the Circumcision which came from
Gaul. This was suppressed in 1969 and 1 January is again celebrated as the feast of the Mother of God.

Evidence of the veneration of Mary can be found in the oldest
strata of the liturgy of Advent in the Roman rite (of which more
will be said in chapter 9.

In the second half of the sixth century, the liturgical season of
Advent appeared and later on in the third week, on the fast days
of Wednesday and Friday, the gospels of the Annunciation and
the Visitation were read on those days respectively. This liturgical arrangement at this time could be said to witness to a grow-
ing devotion to the Blessed Virgin. In Spain, where the season of
Advent was kept earlier than in Rome, a feast of the Expectation
of Mary was celebrated on 18 December. In Gaul, at Tours, there

was a feast of the Blessed Virgin Mary in the sixth century; it was observed on 18th January.

Notes

1. For the history of the first feast or feasts of Mary I have relied on Bernard Capelle, 'La Fête de la Vierge á Jérusalem au Ve Siécle', in *Travaux Liturgiques* III, pp. 281-301 (Mont-César, Louvain, 1967, and also *Muséon*, 1945, pp. 1-33). See also *The Church at Prayer*, IV, ed. A. G. Martimort (ET, London, 1985, pp. 132-137).

2. See P. Jounel, *Le Culte des Saints du Latran et du Vatican au XIIe Siécle* (Rome, 1977), pp. 120-122.

3. *The Church at Prayer*, IV, p. 133.

CHAPTER 3

Mary the Mother of God

Solemnity 1 January, Octave Day of Christmas

From the title of this feast of St Mary it can be seen that this is the great western celebration of Mary, *Theotokos*, the Mother of God. This is its essential meaning as is indicated by its very position in the Calendar. It is the feast of the Mother who brought forth the redeemer of the world and, as such, she is seen to be more closely associated with him than any other human being and her relationship with him is the root and source of all his dignity, honour and grace. It is also the oldest feast of St Mary in the Calendar of the church of the Roman rite,[1] appearing as it does in the seventh century Gregorian Sacramentary. Yet is was overshadowed and then obscured by the feast of the Circumcision of our Lord Jesus Christ which came from Gaul (France) and, since the gospel of that feast mentions the name of Jesus, which became a separate and very popular feast in the fifteenth century that element too came to be emphasised. In the Mass formulary of the 1970 missal there is also a reminder that 1 January is New Year's Day.

One consequence of this is that it is not entirely satisfactory. After all, the feast is about the Motherhood of Mary and we can trace it in various texts of the day. The entrance antiphon conflates two texts of Isaiah, 6:1-7, from the Night Mass of Christmas: 'A light will shine on us this day, the Lord is born for us; he shall be called Wonderful God, Prince of peace...,' and the alternative entrance chant is explicit about the motherhood: 'Hail, holy Mother! The child to whom you gave birth is the king of heaven and earth for ever'. This is reflected in the opening prayer which will be considered lower down. The first reading, Numbers 6:22-27, is the Aaronic blessing and seems to refer to the New Year/Holy Name themes. However, we should remember that 'name' in the Old Testament means God himself and 'blessing' means the communication of a gift by God: 'May the Lord bless you and keep you/May the Lord let his face shine upon you/... This is how they are to call my name down upon the sons of Israel...', that is, the whole people of Israel. This is followed by psalm 66 with the expanded message of salvation: 'O God, be gracious and bless us/ and let your face shed its light upon us/ So will your ways be known upon earth/ and all nations your *saving help*'. This salvation was brought to the human race by Jesus who is Saviour. This theme is carried forward by the second reading, Galatians 4:4-7. The time of salvation has come, God has sent his Son, born of a woman, and though himself subject to the Law he came to redeem those under the Law. By his coming and redeeming work he makes us sons and daughters of God, indwelt by the Holy Spirit so that we can call God 'Abba', Father. Mary in the tradition of the church is the 'woman' who also was indwelt by the Holy Spirit and was thus closely associated with Jesus from the very beginning of his existence as a human being in this world. Moreover, she is the servant (*doulé*) of the Saviour-God, as she calls herself in the Magnificat.

The gospel is that of the Second Mass of Christmas Day with the addition of verse 21. It is the Octave Day of Christmas and here are Joseph and Mary by the side of the manger in which Jesus lay; here are the shepherds, verifying what they had been told and praising God for what they saw while Mary was pondering the great happenings of the night. Eight days later she was also present when, as writers through the ages have liked to observe, there was the first shedding of the Saviour's blood, and the day he received the sacred name Jesus which means 'God saves'. The last verse of the gospel seems to recall the former feast of the Circumcision when it formed the whole gospel of the day. This, however, may be fortuitous, as Luke 2:16-21 was the gospel of the feast of Mary the Mother of God in the earliest lectionary of the eighth century. It serves to remind us that incarnation and redemption are closely related to one another and are not to be sharply divided. As French theologians from the seventeenth century onwards liked to say, the whole of Christ's life from birth to resurrection was redemptive.

The redemption/salvation theme is found in other texts of the day which we will now consider. There is first the ancient and closely wrought opening prayer which is not easy to translate:

> God our Father, author of life,
> may we always profit by the prayers
> of the Virgin Mother Mary,
> for you bring us salvation
> through your Son, who lives and reigns….

Here Mary is seen as the Mother of the Redeemer of whom she is the servant, praying now in heaven that we may open our hearts to the saving love of her son who brings us life. In the prayer over the gifts, the feast of this day together with that of Christmas is 'the beginning of salvation' and we ask that it may be brought to fulfilment in us. A similar message is to be found in the prayer after communion when we proclaim Mary 'the Mother of Christ and the Mother of the Church' and pray that through our communion with her son we may be brought to salvation. This is obviously a post-Vatican II composition, reflecting the teaching of the *Constitution on the Church*, chapter 8, for which see chapter 1 of this book.

When we turn to the *Divine Office*, we move into a world that reflects ideas which take us to the eastern church of Byzantium whence came so much Marian devotion and so many texts of our liturgy. Right at the beginning of First Vespers (EP 1) we meet an antiphon that has a special character:

> O wondrous exchange! The creator of the human race, taking to himself our human nature, was born of the Virgin; he appeared among us as a man without human father and has generously bestowed on us his divine nature.

The original is Greek of course and one phrase, 'taking to himself human nature,' is found in a work of St Cyril of Alexandria (+444) and a very similar phrase is to befound in a sermon of Pope St Leo (+461) in Latin: *'animatum corpus sumens'* where Leo has '*templum*' for '*corpus*'. These perhaps tedious linguistic details show that the church of the east and the west were at one in this matter, not surprisingly because this was the century of the great Christological councils (Ephesus and Chalcedon). It also illustrates the close relationship between Jesus, the Son of God, and his mother, Mary. The Latin text reads '*procedens homo sine semine*', literally, 'coming forth without human seed', which is a way of speaking of the virginal conception and birth. From this we are led to the 'wondrous exchange', which in the Greek could be translated as 'the astonishing exchange'. Jesus Christ took our human nature so that he might communicate to us his divine nature. As the Fathers of the east and the west said over and over again, by the incarnation we are made sons and daughters of God and are 'divinised' or 'deified', sharing even now the divine nature (cf. 2 Pet 1:4).

The next two antiphons, also of Greek provenance, are rather different in style and call for a little exegesis.

> When you (Jesus) were born ... of the Virgin, then were the scriptures fulfilled: "You came down like rain on the fleece to save the human race. We praise you, our God."

Unfortunately the *Divine Office* (1, p. 286) translates '*Vellus*' (fleece) as 'earth' (apparently thinking of Deut 32:2), thus missing the ancient typology the antiphon refers to. It evokes the ancient story of Gideon who saved his people from the Medianites and who sought a sign from God that his efforts would be supported by him. He laid a fleece on the threshing floor and prayed that if it was wet the next morning he would know that God was with him. This is what occurred. Not yet satisfied he tried again, reversing the process; if the fleece remained dry and the ground wet he would be assured. And so it was (Jdg 6:36-40).

The church of the east and the west saw in this some sort of indication of the coming of the Son of God to the Virgin of Nazareth; the falling in silence of the dew on the fleece was a symbol of the mysterious conception and birth of Jesus from Mary. It may seem an odd form of typology but it reveals something of the de-

vout and poetic sensibility of an earlier age. Equally unexpected
is the typology of the third antiphon:

> Moses gazed at the thornbush; it was burnt though not con-
> sumed. Here was a sign of your ever praiseworthy virginity.
> Mother of God, pray for us.

The bush that burns but is not consumed is seen as a sign of the
perpetual virginity of Mary. This is the way the church of the
east and the west read the Bible: the Old Testament was full of
foreshadowings, 'types', of persons and events in the New. So it
was that the incident that concerned Moses could be interpreted
as of Mary's virginity. To us it may seem very strange yet that is
how earlier Christians drew out of the Bible, as they thought,
new things and old. What is common to all three antiphons is
that the virginity of Mary is closely associated with her motherhood, the motherhood of Jesus, the Son of God. As in so much of
the early liturgies (as in the New Testament itself), the motherhood is the root of all her graces. Because she was to be the
Mother of God she was saved from sin at the first moment of her
conception; because she was chosen to give birth to the Son of
God, his conception and birth were virginal, and because of the
bodily bond with her son she was exalted to heaven at the end of
her life. And because she was closer to her son than any other
creature we seek the help of her prayers. The feast of 1 January is
a celebration of Mary *Theotokos* in all the richness of her graces
and privileges.

Not surprisingly it has also a strongly christological character, as
is made clear by the antiphon to the *Benedictus* at Morning
Prayer, a text that is not without its difficulties:

> Today a wonderful mystery is proclaimed: something new
> has taken place; God has become man; he remained what he
> was and has taken that which he was not, and though the
> two natures remain, he is one.

That is the translation in the *Divine Office* (I.254) with two small
changes. It poses one or two questions. The somewhat flat
phrase, 'something has taken place' is in the original and in the
Latin of the *Liturgia Horarum* '*innovantur naturae*', 'natures are

renewed'. How can the divine nature be renewed? That there is a difficulty here can be seen not only from the paraphrase in the *Divine Office*, but from the text in the *Festal Menaion*[2] of the Byzantine liturgy for the feast of the *Theotokos* (26 December), where we find it translated as 'nature is made new'. The best we can do, I think, is to say that the Divine Person began to live a *mode of existence* (in the flesh, in this world) that he had not experienced before.

Likewise, though the translation (a free one) of the phrase 'though the two natures remain, he is one' may seem to make things clear, it is not what either the Latin or the Greek say. There we find, 'suffering neither confusion nor division' which is part of the definition of the Council of Chalcedon which was perhaps worth saving. It is not without interest to learn that the antiphon was extracted from a sermon preached by St Gregory Nazianzen at Constantinople in 379, where the feast of Christmas had recently been introduced from the west. In another sermon, 'On the Holy Lights' (Epiphany), very similar words are also to be found and may be regarded as a commentary on the antiphon:

> What was done? What was the great mystery? An innovation was made upon nature and God is made man... The Son of God deigns to become and to be the Son of Man; not changing what he was but assuming what he was not (for he is full of love for mankind) that the Incomprehensible might be comprehended, conversing with us....[3]

Whatever modern Christians may think of these very theological texts, they bear witness to the deep reflections of a saint which, in council and liturgy, the church has made her own. Perhaps we are inclined to take the event of the incarnation too much for granted. As St Gregory and the antiphons themselves suggest, it was and is a very great mystery and they should draw us on to reverent contemplation.

From other parts of the office of the day we find that the feast is very much a celebration of the motherhood of Mary. The invitatory of the Office of Readings (or Morning Prayer) reads: 'Let us celebrate the motherhood of the Virgin Mary and worship her son' and all three antiphons of the office make this clear:

A root has sprung from Jesse, a star has risen from Jacob, a Virgin has brought forth a Saviour. We praise you our God.

Here is a nice combination of Isaiah 11:1, Numbers 24:17 and Luke 1:33, 2:11.

Mary has given birth to our saviour. Seeing him John cried out, 'Here is the Lamb of God who takes away the sins of the world.'

The coming of the Son of God in the flesh is the beginning of salvation, a theme strongly marked in all the Christmas liturgy.

Mary gave birth to the King. Eternal is his name. With the joy of a mother she combined the honour of a virgin. The world has never seen its like and never will again.

This last sentence is from a poem by Sedulius Scottus (9th century): 'Nec primam similem visa est, nec habere sequentem'. The introit of the former Mass of the Common of the Blessed Virgin Mary, *Salve sancta parens*, was also lifted from another poem by him. The former phrase gives an approximate date of the antiphon. These details apart, this last antiphon evokes something of the wonder and the reverence that the church and its preachers had for the great mystery of the Word becoming flesh through the co-operation of Mary who was chosen by God to be his mother.

Notes

1. Gregory of Tours (+594) records that a feast of the Assumption of the Blessed Virgin Mary was kept in Gaul in the sixth century.

2. *The Festal Menaion*, translated by Mother Mary and Archbishop Kallistos Ware (London, 1969), 291.

3. Trans. *Nicene and Post-Nicene Fathers*. (Michigan, USA, 1974). Second series, vol. 7, Oratio 39, xiii, p. 356. The translator has seen the difficulty about *'innovantur naturae'* and has paraphrased it: 'an innovation is made upon nature'. In yet another sermon Gregory plays on the word 'Being': (He was) Being and eternally Being, of the eternal Being... for our sake (he is) also Becoming, that he who gives us our being might also give us our Well-being... or restore us by his incarnation when by wickedness we had fallen away from well-being'. (*Oratio* 38, iii, vol. 7, p. 345).

CHAPTER 4

The Presentation of the Lord

Solemnity, 2 February

For many centuries, this feast was called the Purification of the Blessed Virgin Mary. In 1970, its title was changed to the Presentation of the Lord, its original name that also emphasises its original meaning, as we shall see. Immediately, we can see that the change of title harmonises the celebration with all the great feasts of Mary which associate her closely with her son. In the rite as it now is, there is a nice balance between the two themes. Its origin is to be found in Jerusalem towards the end of the fourth century. There is a vivid description of its celebration in the travelogue of the lady Egeria who made a long tour to the Holy Places and ended up in Jerusalem.[1]

On the fortieth day after the Epiphany, the people went to the church of the *Anastasis* (the Resurrection) and there celebrated the feast with 'special magnificence, as at the feast of Easter.' The gospel of the day was Luke 2:22-40 (as now) and, as was the custom in Jerusalem, there was much preaching by the presbyters and the bishop. Then the 'holy mysteries' were celebrated. Although the liturgy in fourth century Jerusalem was very mobile (the people went from one holy place to another, especially in Holy Week), there was, it seems, no procession and no mention of candles. From Jerusalem the celebration of the feast spread to Antioch and then to Constantinople where it was called *Hypapante*, 'The *meeting* of our great Saviour with Simeon the Just when the latter took him in his arms'.[2] The Emperor, who took part in the procession, walked barefoot.

The feast was celebrated in Rome in the seventh century, introduced it seems by Pope Sergius I, who may have known it in Antioch where he was born. He was certainly responsible for the procession which made its way from the Forum to the church of St Mary Major, the people carrying candles and the pope wearing black vestments which in Rome were always the sign of penitence. There are those who remember that until 1970 the celebrating clergy wore purple vestments. The reason for this and the Emperor's barefootedness is thought to be that the feast, or at least the procession, replaced and ousted an old pagan festival, though this is not certain.

In Gaul the feast was called the Purification of the Blessed Virgin Mary, no doubt under influence of Luke 2:22, but Greek influence (probably via Spain) is also observable. During the procession, certain antiphons were sung in Greek as well as in Latin and one, the *Adorna thalamum tuum*, in a very garbled translation. Hitherto there had been no blessing of candles. This is first found in Germanic lands and was adopted by Rome only in the twelfth century. It was secondary rite, as it is now again.

The question, however, arises whether this feast is simply a historical commemoration of the gospel record or is it something more. The title *Hypapante* puts us on the way to discovering a deeper meaning. According to the gospel, there was indeed a 'meeting' of Mary, the Child and Joseph with the holy man Simeon in the Temple, but this 'meeting' was full of symbols. The Temple was the symbol, almost one could say the sacrament-sign of the people of the old Covenant, and here is Jesus being brought to it so that all that was necessary according to the Law could be done. Jesus was the first-born and had to be redeemed; so we have the paradox: the Redeemer is being redeemed. The liturgy (see Office of Readings, Ex 13:1-3, 11-16) and the gospel of the day are aware of this. The theme of salvation, redemption, is very strong in the latter: Exodus is quoted, Simeon is awaiting 'the consolation of Israel' and he speaks of the salvation he now sees, and he foretells the child's redeeming work: he is set for 'the falling and rising of many', and the prophetess Phanuel spoke of him 'to all who were looking for the redemption of Israel'.

But what of the Temple? Jesus was coming to the people of Israel, of which the Temple was the symbol, and he would offer to those people salvation and some would accept it and some would refuse it. The Temple was also the place of sacrifice, and the salvation of all, whether Jew or Gentile, would be brought about by the sacrifice of the Lord of the Temple, offering himself on the altar of the cross, or as the early Christian tradition had it, on the altar of his own body (See Jn 2:22).

To sum up, the Presentation in the Temple was the first meeting of Jesus the Saviour with his people, his own people, the people of the Old Testament to whom were given the promises, the Law and the Temple-worship, and of whom 'according to the flesh' he was descended (cf. Rom 9:4, 5).

As the Christian revelation and the liturgy make clear, the covenant, the sacrifices and the Temple have been transcended by the new covenant, by the one sacrifice of the Saviour (cf. scripture reading, Evening Prayer 1: Heb 10:5-7), and by the church which is the new temple 'not made with hands', the spiritual house (or the house of the Spirit) of which there is a new priesthood who offer 'spiritual sacrifices' through Jesus Christ the High Priest (cf. 1 Pet 2:5-9).[3]

For the liturgy then, the sense of the feast is the meeting of the community of the church with Jesus Christ, its Saviour, or perhaps closer to the texts of the day, it is the *encounter* of the Christian people with their Redeemer. So we pray that 'we who carry these candles (the symbols of Christ) into your church come with joy to the light of glory', that is to Christ who is the Light. In the entrance chant to the Mass (only used when there is no procession) we find the words '*Suscepimus, Deus, misericordiam tuam in medio templi tui…*' which should be translated, 'We *welcome* your love, O God, in the midst of your temple' (and not 'we *ponder* your love'), because the church was and still is using the old Latin psalter in this place and saw in it the theme of the encounter of God's people in the church with the Christ. Underlying the Opening Prayer of the Mass is the same theme:

> Almighty, everliving God,
> on this day your only begotten son
> was presented in the temple,
> in flesh and blood like ours:

purify us in mind and heart
that we may *meet* you in your glory.
(Translation *Divine Office*, 1. p. 130).

The matter may be put like this: The Lord Jesus is coming and
renewing his presence in the assembly of the church so that its
members may be renewed by the grace that he communicates to
them. As always, he offers himself to us and it is for us to respond with faith and love. To echo the prayer, 'purification' or
deliverance from sin is an on-going process and this feast is a
step towards the final encounter with God who will welcome us
for the sake of his Son.[4] This is suggested too by a typological
reading of the prophet Malachi (3:1-4) which is the first lection of
the Mass: 'The Lord God says this: Look, I am going to send my
messenger (John the Baptist) to prepare a way before me. And
the Lord you are seeking will suddenly enter his temple; and the
angel of the covenant whom you are longing for, yes, he is coming...'. He will appear among the people, he will purify the
priesthood and then the offering of all will be welcomed by the
Lord. Malachi was thinking of the Day of the Lord, an event that
would happen at some unknown time. It would be preceded by
a coming of the Lord which Malachi could only dimly discern,
but there will be the final day of the Lord when we shall meet
him and, as we pray, we will be welcomed by him into eternal
habitations.

The meeting aspect of the feast is well illustrated by the extract
from the homily of Sophronius of Jerusalem (+638) which is to
be found in the Office of Readings (*Divine Office* 1: pp. 126-7).

'Let us all run to meet him, we who honour and venerate the
mystery of the Lord ...Let us go out to meet him with eager
minds...' carrying candles. 'We add to this the bright shining
of candles... we show forth the divine splendour of the coming of him who made all things bright. The chaste Virgin
Mother of God bore in her arms the true light... We must
hurry out to meet him who is truly light... This is the mystery
we celebrate, that the light has come into the world and has
given it light when it was shrouded in darkness... So now we
go with lamps in our hands and hasten bearing lights show-

ing both that the light has shone upon us, and signifying the glory which is to come to us through him. Therefore let us all run together to meet God'.

It is thus that Sophronius sums up the 'mystery' of the feast. Meeting, light, the light that is Christ borne in the arms of Mary to dispel the darkness of sin, light answering light in the hands of the Christian people which reflects the Light who shines in the hearts of the redeemed; all this is expressed in the short space of the homily.

As has been indicated above, St Mary is more prominent in the Office than the Mass and it is in the former that are preserved fragments of the great antiphon that is sung in full in the Byzantine Office and used to be sung in the procession before Mass. I refer to the *Adorna thalamum tuum*, 'Zion prepare your marriage chamber; see your king, the Christ, is coming to you' (Ev. Pr. ant. 2; Off. Readings, Resp. 1). This is but one phrase of a text of great beauty and considerable theological depth. Some further account of it is called for.

'In the antiphon, *Adorna thalamum tuum*... Mary herself is presented as the new Temple, the bridal room of the Lord... "Adorn thy bridal chamber, O Zion, and welcome Christ the King; salute Mary, the heavenly gate. For she has been made the throne of the cherubim and she carries the King of glory. A cloud of light is the Virgin who has borne the morning star." Simeon, taking him in his arms, proclaimed to the peoples: "This is the Lord of life and death and the Saviour of the world." In this Greek text Mary is "the throne of the cherubim" (cf. psalm 79) who over-shadowed the Mercy Seat in the Temple. She has replaced the Mercy Seat and is now bringing "the Lord of life and death, the Saviour of the world". She is "the cloud of light" for she too had been overshadowed by the power of the Most High who in the Old Testament made his presence known in the cloud, as on Mount Sinai. In this antiphon Mary is a figure or model of the new temple, the church, and she first is the bridal chamber where the first meeting between the Son of God and the human race took place. Furthermore, she is the mother of the Saviour and associates herself with his saving work by presenting, offering him, to his Father'.[5]

As said above, in the Song of Simeon there is a foreshadowing of the passion and resurrection of Jesus. He was destined for the falling and rising of many and, as we know, in his life he was rejected by some and accepted by others. As he himself said, he was a cause of division and his very passion, death and resurrection have been rejected through the ages. The redeeming work of Jesus and the role of Mary are reflected in a troparion of the Great Vespers of the Byzantine rite:

> Hail, O Theotokos, Virgin full of grace: for from thee has shone forth the Sun of Righteousness, Christ the Lord, giving light to those in darkness. Be glad also, thou righteous Elder (Simeon), for thou has received in thine arms the Deliverer of our souls, who bestows on us resurrection.[6]

After this consideration of these many texts of the liturgy of the day, it is clear that the Presentation of the Lord unfolds what is implicit in the incarnation that we celebrate on Christmas Day.

Notes

1. See *Egeria's Travels*, trans. John Wilkinson with notes, SPCK, 1971.

2. See *The Church at Prayer*, ed. A. G. Martimort, Eng. trans. IV, pp. 88-90 (Geoffrey Chapman, 1985).

3. The terms *oikos pneumatikos* (spiritual house) and *thusias pneumatikas*. (spiritual sacrifices) of 1 Peter 2:5 are difficult to translate. 'Pneumatikos' in the NT does not necessarily mean 'disembodied' or 'non-material'. It usually refers to the Holy Spirit who, in this context, we may say is dwelling in the church. It is the church of the Spirit. Likewise the 'spiritual sacrifices' are sacrifices offered in the Spirit, or by the power of the Spirit, and some commentators have seen in the term a reference to the holy eucharist.

4. This sentence is taken from my *The Coming of the Lord* (Kevin Mayhew, 1990), p. 89.

5. This whole passage is taken from *The Coming of the Lord*, p. 89 and the texts of the Byzantine Office from *The Festal Menaion*, trans. Mother Mary and Kallistos (Ware) (Faber and Faber, 1969) pp. 416-417.

6. *Ibid.*

CHAPTER 5

The Annunciation of the Lord

Solemnity, 25 March

Though since the revised Roman Calendar of 1969, this feast is now definitively a feast of the Lord, it was long considered to be a feast of the Blessed Virgin Mary. Indeed it was regarded as the chief feast of Mary, a celebration of her motherhood of the Divine Child which is the root doctrine of her status in salvation history. Yet its celebration was somewhat overshadowed by Lent when the feast was almost always kept in both the eastern and the western church. How was it that the date of such a feast should have been fixed on 25 March?

In the third century there was a good deal of discussion about the date of Christ's birth. One factor was the Christian interpretation of Psalm 18. Christ was seen as the *Sun* rising at one end of the sky (the east) and moving to its setting in the west. As has been said elsewhere, he was regarded as a bridegroom coming forth from his tent which, in the Greek and Latin psalter, was translated as marriage bed (*thalamus*). It was a foreshadowing of the birth of Christ coming forth from Mary's womb. It is a very ancient interpretation. A mosaic under St Peter's, Rome, of the third century, depicts the *Christos-helios*, Christ as the sun. This understanding of Psalm 18 (and other texts) drew the Christian attention to equinoxes and solstices of the year, and looking into Luke 1:26 some came to the conclusion that John the Baptist was conceived at the autumn equinox and, since Christ was conceived six months after John, therefore in the spring equinox, the Annunciation of Christ occurred at that time, i.e. in the month of March, and with a further refinement, on 25th of that month.[1]

If we turn to the texts of the former Mass and compare them with those of the present formulary, we see that they have undergone a decisive re-orientation. It is now definitely a feast of the Lord but with appropriate attention to Mary. In the former Mass it was the wedding ode, Psalm 44, that was exploited. The introit, the gradual (and tract) and the Alleluia verses (for Eastertide) were all from that psalm and applied to Mary. Thus, for the introit the verse from the psalm, '*Your face* shall the rich people seek...' (*Vultum tuum*), is applied to Mary, and we find the same thing in the gradual: 'Grace is poured upon your lips because God has blessed you for evermore', which in Hebrews (1:9) is applied to Christ! Clearly this would not do and the revisers took another line, more in keeping with the nature of the feast. Their work can be seen first in the prayers of the Mass.

The opening prayer is substantially that of the former missal, but it has removed the phrase about the annunciation of the angel. It runs, however, like this: 'It was God's saving plan (his will) that the Word should take flesh in the womb of the Virgin Mary; we confess our faith in the Redeemer who is both God and man and pray that we may share his diyine nature.' Mary, as all through the texts of the feast, is the Mother of the Son of God who is our redeemer. Once again incarnation and salvation go together.

In the prayer over the offerings (which replaces the former one) there is the interesting statement that the church had its origins in the incarnation and we, (the church) pray that God will accept our offering as we celebrate the mystery of his only Son made flesh. The prayer after communion (formerly that over the offerings) prays that through the Son 'conceived by the Virgin Mary', and through his resurrection, we may come to everlasting happiness. These prayers then are very comprehensive, recalling conception, birth, redemption and resurrection while giving Mary her role in all this process.

Mary's part is unfolded in the first reading (Is 7:10-14) and in Luke 1:26-38. The Isaian text has its difficulties and a few words of explanation seem called for. Judah is under the threat of invasion from the rulers of the northern kingdom, called Israel, and of Damascus, who want to force king Ahaz into an alliance with the Assyrians. Instead of trusting in God, Ahaz has opted for the alliance. In the mind of the prophet, this will be disastrous for Judah: attack will lead to the destruction of the Davidic dynasty in which is vested the Messianic hope. Isaiah, moved by

God, gives the sign the fulfilment of which will prove to negative the king's lack of trust in God. In spite of him, the succession
will be secured: 'The maiden is with child and will soon give
birth'. Many scholars think that the 'child' would be the good
king, Hezekiah, who will eventually reign. Then there is the
question of 'the maiden', translated in the Latin Vulgate as 'virgin'.
The Hebrew word *'almah'* means a young woman of marriage-
able age, whether she is married or not. But the word has a history.
In the Greek, pre-Christian, translation of the Old Testament
(the Septuagint) *'almah'* is translated as *'parthenos'* which usually
means 'virgin'. Some scholars are of the opinion that the rabbis
of the second century BC saw a Messianic meaning in the
promises and were willing to accept *'parthenos'*. The birth of the
Messiah would be an extraordinary event. Matthew, the evangelist, simply took over this translation (1:23) though it is not entirely clear that he intended the *word* simply to be a *proof* of the
virginal conception.[2] He may have wanted to show that Jesus
was of the line of David.

Likewise, 'Emmanuel... God is with us' did not have the force in
the Old Testament it has when it appears in Matthew. Israel as a
whole is sometimes called 'son of God', and in Psalm 88 (89): 27
David calls God his father who makes him his first-born. To this
we may add that the 'son' of Psalm 2 and the 'Lord' of Psalm 109
(110) is not the Son of God in the full sense of the term as in the
New Testament. It is the Christian church that has seen the full
sense of these and other texts.

The historicity of the infancy gospels has been vigorously dis-
cussed for many years, but this is not the place or the occasion to
do so. Let us rather see Luke 1:26-38 as the evangelist's medita-
tion on the stupendous event of the conception of the Son of God
in the womb of the Blessed Virgin Mary. His language and his
treatment suggest that it is a very solemn proclamation, precisely
the Annunciation *to* Mary that she was to be the mother of the
Son of God. Everything in this passage indicates that Luke was
aware that God was breaking into this world in a new way to
save humankind from their sins (cf. 1:68, 69). 'In the sixth
month' (omitted by the Lectionary) the messenger Gabriel,
whose name means the power of God, was sent to the virgin of

Nazareth called Mary, who was engaged to Joseph of 'the house
of David' in whose line God had vested the promise of the
Messiah. Gabriel is the one sent perhaps because he was associated with certain Messianic prophecies and acts of divine power
in the Old Testament (see Daniel, 8 and 9). He is now going to
proclaim the coming of the Messiah. Gabriel gives a joyful greeting, 'Rejoice', he has good news to bring, good news to the one
who is called 'highly favoured', engraced, for when God shows
favour he gives a gift, the gift we call grace. 'The Lord is with
you', a common enough greeting (cf. Ruth 2:4) but here it has a
special solemnity and significance. Mary is 'the highly favoured'
of the Lord but the Lord will be with her in a new and utterly un-
foreseen way. Mary is afraid and disturbed as Daniel was (8:17)
by the presence of Gabriel who represents the all-Holy-God and
in a sense makes him present, here first by his word. There is no
need to fear, she has found favour with God, she is loved by
God, she is endowed with a gift to prepare her for her high destiny.

Then comes the proclamation that is echoed by the exceedingly
great joy of the Christmas gospel: 'You are to conceive and bear
a son, and you must name him Jesus. He will be great and will
be called the Son of the Most High. The Lord will give him the
throne of David; he will rule over the House of Jacob for ever
and his kingdom will have no end'. He is the heir of David, the
promises made to the house of David are being fulfilled in him
(cf. Psalms 2 and 109) but, far transcending the promises, he will
be the Son of the Most High. It is because of this that his kingdom will never have an end.

To Mary's humble question, 'How can this come about...?'
Gabriel in reply repeats his message and makes a great theological
statement: 'The Holy Spirit will come upon you and the power
of the Most High will overshadow you and the Holy One born
of you will be the Son of God.' Jesus, the Saviour, is proclaimed
God's Son, and as we read in Matthew, he will save his people
from their sins. To her high destiny, to her high vocation, Mary,
entrusting herself wholly to the Lord, however much or little she
understands of it, gives her consent: 'Let it be to me according to
your word', as the Revised Standard Version has it. Mary, now

unquestioningly submits herself totally to the creative word of
God. So she becomes, as it were, the Ark of the Covenant, the
Mercy seat where God appeared, she is the *Shekina* where God
dwells, she is made holy so that she can give birth to the Holy
One of the Father.

The theme of salvation is high-lighted by what is the most con-
spicuous addition to the Mass of the day: the insertion of Psalm
39:7-11 and the second reading, Hebrews 10:4-10. Here Jesus
Christ, Son of God and son of Mary, is the Redeemer who comes
to do the will of his Father, 'Here I am Lord! I come to do your
will' (the response to the psalm), and in the extract from the
Letter to the Hebrews we read what is a quotation from the
psalm: 'As it was commanded in the scroll of the book/God,
here I am! I am coming to do your will' (the author is quoting
from the Greek psalter). This is an expression of the total giving
of Jesus to his Father for us and for our salvation which he did
with an immensity of love that is beyond our comprehension.
As we read in the gospel of St John (4:34), Jesus said to his disciples, 'My food is to do the will of the one who sent me', and to
complete the redeeming work for which he was sent. We can
ponder on these texts at length, but here they remind us that
Jesus is Lord, that he is the Son of God, that he is the Word made
flesh (cf. gospel acclamation), but that even on this feast he is
Saviour and Redeemer who, in the words of Jeremiah, loves us
with an everlasting love. With that same love he loved his mother,
who is the *Alma Redemptoris Mater* (the dear mother of the
Redeemer), and who loved him in return.

When we turn to the Office of the day we find that the incarna-
tion of the Son of God and the role of Mary are kept in balance.
In Evening Prayer 1 (antiphon 1) there is the Messianic text from
Isaiah 11:1:

> A shoot will spring from the stock of Jesse,
> a new shoot will grow from his roots.

It is applied to Mary, no doubt on account of the Vulgate translation; 'shoot' in the second line is translated '*flos*', flower, (or even
rose as in some popular carols). In fact both lines (an example of

Hebrew parallelism) refer to the descendant of Jesse, David, as
the next line indicates: 'On him will rest the spirit of the Lord…'.

However, perhaps even Jerome (the translator) regarded the
'*flos*' as a prophecy of the one who would give birth to the
Messiah, as in the liturgy, the psalm that follows suggests: 'To
the childless wife he (God) gives a home/and gladdens her
heart with children.' Much in the Office reminds one of the office of Christmas. Thus the canticle is Philippians 2:6-11, the
great hymn of the incarnation, the passion, death and exaltation
of Jesus. The short reading from 1 John 1:1,2 seems to make the
incarnate Word present to us:

> What has existed from the beginning,
> what we have heard and seen with our eyes,
> what we have gazed upon
> and touched with our hands,
> The Word who is life.

For the responsory that follows we have the reference to the star
that rises over Jacob (Num 24:17), combined with the shoot of
Jesse. The antiphon for the Magnificat recalls to us the work of
the Holy Spirit in the coming of the Son of God from Mary: 'The
Holy Spirit will come upon you…'.

The concluding prayer sums up the celebration very satisfactorily:
'Lord God, by your saving plan your Word truly took our flesh
in the womb of the Virgin Mary. Grant that we who profess our
faith in our Redeemer as true man, may be made like him in his
divine nature.'

In the Office of Readings, the Messianic Psalms 2 and 44 are
used, as well as Psalm 18, on which we have commented above.
The antiphons chosen show that the christological interpretation
is intended. Thus for Psalm 18 the antiphon is: 'When he came
into the world, he said: "You have prepared a body for me…"'
(Heb 10:5) and for Psalm 44: 'God showed how much he loved
us by sending his only Son into the world, so that we might have
life through him' (1 Jn 4:9). The Messianic theme is continued in
the first reading (1 Chron 17:1-15) concerning the establishment
of the line of David and the building of the Temple by Solomon:

'He will build a house for me, and I will establish his throne
for ever. I will be his father and he shall be my son; I will not
take my steadfast love from him ...' This is followed by the responsory, Luke 1:26, 27 from which, oddly, the words describing
Joseph as 'of the house of David' are omitted. The second
reading, a longish extract from St Leo's famous letter to
Flavian, Patriarch of Constantinople, which became the
Tomus of the Council of Chalcedon (451), and which with
minor changes became the definitive doctrine of the two natures in the person of Christ, puts the christological nature of
the feast beyond doubt. Mary's role is included in the responsory that follows: 'You will conceive and bear a son, both
God and man. You will be called "Blessed among women"'.

The Marian theme is continued and prominent in the antiphons
of Morning and Evening Prayer which are drawn from Luke 1
and 2. In the light of all the texts of the liturgy, I think we are
justified in saying that the Annunciation is the celebration of
Mary, *Theotokos*, if we give weight to both parts of that word:
Mary gives birth to Jesus (the Son of God) and, in this perspective, the feast is the western parallel of the eastern feast of the
same name. It has resonances of the latter and makes it own contribution soberly but devoutly in the Roman way.

Notes

1. For this theory see Adolf Adam, *The Liturgical Year* (Pueblo, NY, 1979)
p. 123.
2. For the whole text see John L. McKenzie, SJ, *Dictionary of the Bible*
(London, 1965) s.v. 'Emmanuel', p. 234.

CHAPTER 6

The Visitation of the Blessed Virgin Mary

Feast, 31 May

Strange as it may seem, the feast of the Visitation, though a biblical event, had no place in the calendars of the church until the thirteenth century. In the east there was indeed a feast kept on 2 July, of the 'Deposition of the Holy Robe of the Theotokos', at the church of the Blachernae in Constantinople, but this had nothing to do with the Visitation. However, the Franciscans chose this day for the feast when they introduced it into the calendar in 1263. The abortive Council of Basel in 1441 had a special Mass formulary drawn up, and Pope Sixtus IV (+1484), a Franciscan, had another composed. It was not until the Dominican Pope, Pius V (+1572), inserted the feast into the Roman Calendar of 1568 that it was universally observed in the west. Understandably, most of the texts of the Mass and Office are taken from Luke 1:39-56. But we are prompted to ask: is the meaning of the feast simply that Mary was doing an act of charity by visiting Elizabeth and sharing her good news with her who had her own good news to tell? That is one obvious reading of St Luke's story. It is, however, but one part of the infancy gospel which has been carefully wrought so as to convey certain 'theological' statements. There is the annunciation of John to which is set in parallel the annunciation to Mary. There is the description of the birth of John and then, in chapter 2, the account of the birth of Christ. Between them comes the Visitation. These two blocks are mosaics of Old Testament quotations and implicit references that convey of a message of salvation history. As we have seen, the *Benedictus* is a prophetic message of salvation which will be brought about by the 'Son of the Most High'. Out of the bountiful mercy of God, who in his Son will come and visit his people, will come forgiveness. In a previous chapter, we have seen that

47

the annunciation to Mary is a proclamation of salvation through her son, and we recall the words, 'God protects Israel, remembering his mercy, the mercy promised to our fathers…'. The saving mercy of the Most High is going to be made present and effective in a new way in the new kingdom that is beginning to break into the old order. It is this matter, and indeed others (the divine motherhood of Mary and her virginity), that were the concerns of Luke and it was these that he wanted to lay before the people as the revelation of God's ways with his people. The question then arises: is the Visitation narrative outside Luke's presentation of salvation history? From a literary point of view, it is in the same style as the rest of the narratives and it is concerned, I believe, to convey a deeper message than appears on the surface.

As the story is often treated in homilies, the Visitation was a charitable act on the part of Mary: she wanted to be with Elizabeth at the time of her lying-in and the birth of her son.[1] There is a suggestion of this in the choice of the alternative first reading (Rom 12:9-15) which is about love of neighbour. If the story is factual, this cannot be ruled out but we have to remember that the relationship of Elizabeth to Mary is obscure ('kinswomen': *syggenis*), and later the Baptist says that he did not know Jesus (Jn 1:31).

What then is the message? We remember that Elizabeth is the wife of Zechariah, a priest of Temple. As Mary approaches, Elizabeth is filled with the Holy Spirit and feels her child move in her womb. Under the inspiration of the Holy Spirit, she calls Mary, 'the mother of her *Lord*' and proclaims her blessed among women and blessed the fruit of her womb. The author is saying that Elizabeth has full knowledge not only of what had happened to Mary but of its full meaning: She is the mother of One who is God. Mary's reply is not only a hymn of praise for the 'great things' God had done for her and in her but, as we have pointed out above, it is a hymn about salvation: God is her Saviour and his saving mercy reaches from generation to generation, from Abraham down to those who existed in her day, herself, Elizabeth, John the Baptist and all the Jewish people to whom Mary belonged.

The narratives seems to suggest further that Mary, as the Ark of the new Covenant, as the *Shekina*, the 'place' where God dwells, Mary who is bearing the Saviour of the world, approaches John the Baptist and the Saviour sanctifies him in the womb of his mother (cf. Jer 1:5). Thus chosen, he is to go out and proclaim the Saviour as he will do some thirty years later. This is the theme of the *Benedictus* 1:68-79 and the last sentence of the chapter tells us of the Baptist 'who was in the wilderness till the day of his manifestation to Israel'. Then he will preach the gospel of baptism for the taking away of sins and proclaim the coming, and indeed the presence, of the Messiah among the people he was speaking to.

Or perhaps we could say that the new order of salvation was approaching the old order of which the Baptist was the last representative and the herald of the new. As such he was engraced by the 'meeting' with the Messiah through his mother Mary. Once more she is brought into close proximity to the saving work of her son.

Whatever may be thought of this interpretation, Elizabeth's words (or the words the author has put on her lips) are quite extraordinary: 'Blessed are you among women and blessed the fruit of your womb... The mother of the Lord... the infant leaped in my womb for joy... Blessed is she who believed that the promise made her by the Lord would be fulfilled.' This represents a full understanding of all that has gone before in the annunciation to Mary and of the significance of what was occurring at the visitation. This goes far beyond seeing the latter as a mere charitable visit.

Though the first reading of the Mass (Song 2:8-14; 8:6, 7 and see Office of Readings) is not easy to interpret, it seems to support the above view. Modern exegetes see the Song of Songs as simply a (very frank) love poem, hymning the joys of sexual love between man and women. But since Origen (3rd century) it has been seen as an allegorical poem about the love of Christ for his bridal church. This, no doubt, is true also of its use in the liturgy, and it is as such that we must treat of it here.

I hear my Beloved.
See how he comes
leaping on the mountains,
bounding over the hills....

However incongruously, the text seems to be applied to Mary
making her way over the hilly country from Nazareth to 'a town
in Judah' which was near Jerusalem, bearing Jesus in her womb.
The new Jerusalem is approaching the old.

See where he stands
behind our wall,
He looks in at the window,
he peers through the lattice.

Now it is the voice of the Lover we hear:

Come then, my love,
my lovely one come.
For see, the winter is past,
the rains are over and gone.
The flowers appear on the earth....

It is the springtime of the era of salvation which is breaking in on
the world. The voice of the Lover addresses the one who will be
the herald of that salvation, the herald of the Saviour of whom
his Father had sung in the *Benedictus*. But he as yet remains concealed, in the womb of his mother, and he is bidden to come out,
'show your face', as he will do very publicly in the years to come
when he proclaims repentance because (at last) the kingdom is
near.

That the church is involved seems hardly doubtful. The images
change, the persons addressed or intended are not always clear
but the last stanza seems to suggest the union of Christ with his
church, which is a union of unbreakable love:

Love is strong as death,
passion as relentless as Sheol.
...

Love no flood can quench,
no torrents drown.

In this perspective, Mary is the church, the new Temple, bearing Christ coming to the old Temple, the Voice is the voice of Christ speaking to John hidden in the womb of his mother. The Voice is announcing the springtime which John in his turn will proclaim. The love is the redeeming love of Jesus which will bring in the kingdom of which the sign, the symbol and the sacrament is the church made one with Jesus 'who loved us (the human race) and gave himself up as a fragrant offering and sacrifice to God' (Eph 5:2).

That such a view is not so far from probability may be gathered from the words of the Baptist recorded in John 3:29, 30:

> The bride is only for the bridegroom;
> and yet the bridegroom's friend,
> who stands and listens,
> is glad when he hears the bridegroom's voice.
> This same joy I feel, and now it is complete.
> He must grow greater, I must grow smaller.

The bridegroom's friend has heard the voice of the bridegroom and now he must fade away as he is concealed in Herod's prison.

Notes

1. Verse 56, which seems to suggest that Mary went home before the birth, is to be understood as Luke's style, his way of 'signing off': 'this is the end of the story'.

CHAPTER 7

The Assumption of the Blessed Virgin Mary

Solemnity, 15 August

The origins of the feast of the Assumption have been sketched out in chapter 2. It remains for us to examine the liturgical formularies that have been used over the centuries. It is worth doing so, as they show a certain development.

The mass formulary of the 1570 Roman Missal was substantially that of the Gregorian Sacramentary of the late seventh century and of a lectionary of a little later. It is somewhat colourless. Apart from a reference to the departure of Mary from this world (*quam... migrasse cognovimus*) in the prayer over the offerings, and a mention of the Assumption in the prayer after communion, there is nothing particularly appropriate. The introit was *Gaudeamus omnes in Domino* (Let us rejoice in the Lord) which mentioned the Assumption but it was used, with the necessary changes, on non-Marian feasts. Verses from Psalm 44 (45) were used for the gradual. The epistle was from Ecclesiasticus 24, used for feasts of virgins. Mary is regarded as holy Wisdom who takes up her dwelling in Zion and is exalted like a cedar in Lebanon. The gospel was taken from what came to be called the Common of Virgins; Mary, the sister of Martha, sitting at the feet listening to his words was regarded as the model of dedicated and contemplative virgins. To this passage in the seventh century or so was added Luke 11:27-8, 'Blessed is the womb that bore you...' in an attempt to make the reading appropriate to the feast.

The Mass formulary drawn up after the 1950 definition of the Assumption marks a firmer understanding of the content of the feast. The introit now became Apocalypse 12:1: 'A great sign appeared in heaven, a woman clothed with the sun, with the moon under her feet...'. The opening prayer and that over the offerings and the one after communion bear the mark of the definition: 'Mary, the immaculate Mother of the Son, was taken up body and soul to the glory of heaven'. In the prayer over the offerings, the prayer of Mary for us (an ancient theme) is underlined, and after communion we are invited to pray to her whom God has taken up to heaven that she may help us to come to resurrection. Rather surprisingly, the epistle was taken from Judith 13:22; 15:10, largely it would seem on account of the words, 'Blessed are you, daughter, by the Lord God the Most High, blessed are you above all other women on earth.' In view of Judith's gruesome deed and the associations that remain in our minds about her, it does not strike one as an altogether happy choice. The passage, however, ends with the well known verse, long applied to our Lady: 'You are the glory of Jerusalem, the joy of Israel, the honour of your people.' An immense improvement in the Mass formulary of 1970 is the choice of the gospel, Luke 1:41-56, the story of the Visitation, when we hear an echo of the Judith phrase, 'Blessed are you among women...' from the lips of Elizabeth who adds, because 'she is the mother of my Lord'. This is important because in all the tradition concerning the Assumption, the motherhood of Mary is seen as the deepest reason for her exaltation. We find this in a writer of the sixth century, Theotecknos, in his Encomium for the feast of the Assumption (15): 'For if the *God-bearing body* of the holy one knew death it did not suffer *corruption*. But it was saved from corruption and kept free from stain and raised to the heavens... together with her pure and immaculate soul, and is now... higher than the heavens with the exception of God alone...'.[1] This will be elaborated by St John of Damascus (+749) later on.

The gospel now includes the whole of the Magnificat (the former Mass had only part of it) and, if we reflect that it was written down after Mary's death, we can recite it as a hymn of her exaltation:

My soul glorifies the Lord,
my spirit rejoices in God my saviour.

With Mary we glorify the Lord, we rejoice because 'He that is mighty has done great things' for her. He has looked with

favour on his lowly handmaid, the Holy Spirit has overshadowed her and the Holy One born of her is the Son of God. His
saving mercy, his faithful love, has never failed throughout the
generations, he has remembered his mercy shown to Abraham
and his descendants, and now in this eschatological moment it is
extended to her. She, the mother of the Saviour, is now exalted
to heaven.

The opening prayer, the one over the offerings and that after
communion, are the same as in the Mass of 1950. In the first we
ask that God, who raised the sinless Virgin Mary body and soul
to heaven, will set our hearts on the things of heaven and so
come to share her glory. In the second we pray that our hearts
may be filled with love and that we may aspire to be in the presence of God through the Mass and the prayers of Mary. This element of intercession is found again in the third prayer, where
once again we pray that we may be brought to the glory of resurrection. This last theme runs through much of the liturgy of the
day. As the Preface of the Mass has it, Mary's exaltation is the
foreshadowing of our own.

There are several texts in the Vigil Mass and that of the day
which, apart from one, have not been used in the liturgy of the
Assumption before. In the Vigil Mass (to be used only on the
evening before the feast) we find a passage from 1 Chronicles 15,
another from Psalm 131 (132) and a third from 1 Corinthians 15.
These in one way or another can be related through different images: Ark (of the covenant, 1 Chron 15 and Psalm 131), incorruptibility (1 Cor 15:53, 54), sanctuary (Apoc 11:19) and the first
of the redeemed (1 Cor 15:22, 23).

It will, I think, be best to take the Ark image first, as this, strangely,
binds together the other texts. It may be asked what the Ark of
the Covenant has to do with the Assumption of Mary? In the
Fathers of the church (see Theotecknos above) Mary's body was
preserved from corruption because of her own human substance she had given Christ his human nature. The passage from
Chronicles celebrates the retrieval of the Ark and its triumphal
return to Jerusalem after it had been captured by the Philistines.
But the reason for its inclusion here is that the wood of the Ark

was regarded as *incorruptible* (cf. Ex 25:10ff) and in the first feast
of the Assumption (see chapter 2) it was regarded as the symbol
of the incorruptibility of the body of Mary. In the Greek translation of Psalm 131 and in the Latin that is based on it we read:

> Rise up, Lord, to your rest,
> you and the ark of (your) holiness.

The fifth century liturgy of Jerusalem saw the Lord taking up
Mary, the ark of holiness, to her final rest in the glory of heaven.
This psalm has now been inserted into our liturgy (the Vigil
Mass) as the responsorial psalm after the first reading:

> At Ephrata we heard of the ark;
> we found it in the plains of Yearim.
> Let us go to the place of his dwelling,
> let us go to kneel at his footstool.

This is a translation from the Hebrew; hence the difference. But
the verse, 'Go up, Lord, to the place of your rest/you and the ark
of your strength' has unaccountably been omitted. Though not
of course referring in its primary sense to the exaltation of Mary,
it could be used (perhaps as a response) in the Greek-Latin
translation, as it has been by the eastern churches for centuries.

Thirdly, there is in the psalm a Davidic reference: 'Lord, remember David... the Lord swore an oath to David... A son, the fruit
of your body/will I set upon your throne.' Traditionally Mary,
like Joseph, was of the house and line of David (Lk 2:4), and here
Jesus, the fruit of her body, is that 'son'. Because she brought
forth Jesus, the Son of God, she was preserved incorrupt at the
end of her life. It is this consideration, along with the Ark symbol, that has suggested the inclusion in the liturgy of 1
Corinthians 15:54-57: 'This perishable nature has put on imper-
ishability...' and the last but one sentence suggests that in Mary
death has been overcome: 'Death, where is your victory...?' The
victory over death was effected by our Lord Jesus Christ, the son
of Mary, and she was the first beneficiary of the total victory
over death.

We have not, however, finished with the Ark symbol; it is put

before us in the first reading of the Mass of the day: 'The sanctuary of God in heaven opened, and the ark of the covenant could
be seen inside it'. Then follows the figure of the woman: 'A great
sign appeared in heaven: a woman adorned with the sun, standing on the moon, and twelve stars on her head for a crown.' The
inclusion of verse 19 of chapter 11 is an indication that, in the
liturgical context, the 'ark' is meant to be taken with the
'woman' of 12:1. The question is whether the 'woman' is the
church or Mary.

Apocalypse 11:19 seems to be concerned with the end-time
(verse 18: 'The time has now come'), the time of the new Israel,
the time of the Messianic community which with a new covenant
is coming into being.

It is at this time that the woman appears in the shining light of
the sun with the moon at her feet and the stars over her head.
She is an idealised figure best understood as the heavenly and
new Jerusalem, brilliant in the light of God (21:1-4; 10-14), the
twelve stars perhaps symbolising the twelve tribes of Israel (for
the author of the Apocalypse sees the old Israel and the new in
continuity). This woman suffers the pangs of childbirth; she is
bringing forth the new Israel, as the Old Testament foretold. The
'daughter of Zion' suffers the pangs of a woman in labour
(Micah 4:9) which was a conventional metaphor for the bringing
in of the Messianic age (cf. Mt 10:17, Jn 16:1-4). She is giving
birth to the Messiah: 'the woman brought forth a male child into
the world' and the Accuser, the Adversary, is waiting to devour
the child but he is taken up to God and his throne, and the
woman escapes into the desert, a place of refuge where, however,
God is, and there she will remain for an indefinite but a very
long time (1260 days) until the final eschatological fulfilment.
The child is the Messiah, the Christ, and the woman is the
church, and the whole scene, if such it can be called, is the birth
of the new Israel, the new covenant (symbolised by the ark), and
of the coming into the world of the Messiah who, after his passion, death and resurrection, ascends to be with his father.

Commentators are of the opinion that this is the primary meaning of the text but some at least hold that there is a secondary

symbol, Mary, the Mother of Christ. This is true of the use of the passage in the liturgy of the day. The picture of the woman is very striking: she is glorious, standing in the brilliant light of the sun, or, we may say, in the 'glory of God' which fills the heavens with light (cf. Apoc 21:22, 23), and she gives birth to no ordinary child, for the Accuser (Satan) is waiting to destroy him. With this, however, Mary is seen as a figure of the church. As we have seen in an earlier chapter (3) she is the first church; she bore in her womb and gave her substance to him who is the head of the church. She was the first of the redeemed, she was the first believer and, like the (completed) Pauline church, she was without spot or wrinkle.

Above I have said that Mary is the first of the redeemed, and the second reading suggests that she was the first to follow Christ into glory, that is, the first to be taken up to heaven, body and soul, as the completed model of the Christian and the church. This is the sense of the verse: 'Christ as the first-fruits and then, after the coming of Christ, *those who belong to him*' (23). The first to belong to Jesus in life, death and after death is his mother Mary.

Most of the ideas expressed in the texts of the day are summarised and proclaimed in the first part of the eucharistic prayer (the Preface) which is a fine example of prayed theology. We praise and thank God through Jesus Christ because by the divine power the virgin-Mother of God (*Deipara*) has been taken into heaven. There she is shown to be 'the beginning and pattern (or figure) of the church in its perfection'. She is the exemplar of what the church will be when it too is taken up at the end of time, and the 'church', let us not forget, is the people of God. They too will be like Mary, as she is already, whole in body, soul and spirit, and seeing the face of God (cf. 1 Jn 3:2). Because of this the Assumption and exaltation of Mary is the 'sign of hope and comfort' to the people who make their pilgrim way, sometimes painfully, to the glorious vision of God. She is model, figure, exemplar because she had given birth to the Son of God, the Lord of life, and that was the source of her incorruptibility: 'You would not let decay to touch her body.' Mary is the forerunner, the anticipation of what we shall be if, like her, we are faithful

servants of God. We too are destined to be in glory, living life
from its very source, the life of love that *is* God, Father, Son and
Holy Spirit. As Mary experienced a 'resurrection', so shall we
'for since we believe that Jesus died and rose again, even so
through Jesus Christ God will bring with him those who have
fallen asleep' (1 Thess 4:14). The wholeness that was ours at
birth will be restored to us after death though we do not know
when. This is why Mary's Assumption is 'a sign of hope and
comfort' to the Christian people.

In the *Divine Office* of the day, the psalms are from the Common
of the Blessed Virgin Mary and no use is made of Psalm 18:2-7
nor of Psalm 44:11-18, which one would have thought appropriate to the feast. Nor did the revisers think to use anywhere in the
liturgy of the day the oldest prayer of the Assumption in the
Roman liturgy. This is the prayer which begins *Veneranda* and
was recited at the beginning of the procession from the church of
St Hadrian to that of St Mary Major in the seventh century, as
described above in chapter 2. It came from and was perhaps ob-
tained from the eastern church by Pope Sergius I.

> *Veneranda nobis, Domine, huius diei festivitas, in qua sancta Dei*
> *Genetrix mortem subiit temporalem, nec tamen mortis nexibus de-*
> *primi potuit, quae filium tuum Dominum nostrum de se genuit in-*
> *carnatus.*

> It is right, Lord, that we should keep this festal day when the
> holy Mother of God underwent death in this world of time,
> yet the bonds of death had no power over her because from
> the substance of her body she gave flesh to your Son, our
> Lord Jesus Christ.

It is a proclamatory prayer, hailing the mystery of Mary's exaltation. In a short space it says everything that is necessary and it
would be a good thing if it were re-introduced into our liturgy, if
only because it would be a link with the Byzantine church.
There, in the night office, it is a chant called a *Kontakion* from
which the prayer evidently derives:

> Neither the tomb nor death had power over the Theotokos,
> who is ever watchful in her prayers and in whose unfailing
> intercession lies unfailingly hope. For as the Mother of Life

she has been transported into life by him who dwelt within her everlasting womb.[2]

The *Kontakion* and so the prayer have an ancient origin. It is found in Psalm 15:9, 10, which was quoted by St Peter in his address to the crowd after Pentecost when he applied it to the Risen Christ: '... my body will rest secure/for you will not abandon me to Hades/ *or allow your holy one to see corruption.* You have taught me the way of life/and will fill me with joy in your presence' (in Acts 2:25-28). The church in the fifth century saw a parallel between the resurrection-ascension of Christ with the going forth from this world of Mary his Mother. The comparison must not be pressed too far; it is best seen as a reflection of the church on the taking up to heaven of the Blessed Virgin Mary which was an act of God's power. It would seem that this prayer might be used either somewhere in the liturgy of the day (Vigil or Mass of the Day) or in a procession before the eucharist as a solemn beginning to the celebration on the feast day itself.

Notes

1. See *A Catholic Dictionary of Theology* (Edinburgh, 1962), vol. 1, p. 174, s.v. 'Assumption' (H. F. Davies).

2. *The Festal Menaion* (London, 1969), p. 520.

CHAPTER 8

The Nativity of the Blessed Virgin Mary

Feast, 9 September

Nothing is known of the circumstances of the birth of the Blessed Virgin; the gospels have nothing to say on the matter. Early in the second century, however, there were speculations about it and, in an apocryphal gospel called the *Proto-evangelium* of James, we read a story of Mary's conception by Joachim and Anne, her alleged parents. Whether or not this had any influence on the establishment of a feast is uncertain. What we do know is that it had its origin in the eastern part of the church where a church was dedicated to St Anne. This was built on the site of a house in which it was supposed Mary was born. The feast was known in the late fifth century as is evidenced by the hymns of Romanos Melódos which were already popular in about 500 AD.[1]

The feast was introduced into Rome in the seventh century and was one of the four Marian feasts to which Pope Sergius attached a procession. What in fact is celebrated in the feast is not so much the birth of Mary as her divine motherhood. It is this that is apparent in all the texts of the Mass and the Office. This is made clear by the opening prayer of the Mass: 'Lord God, the day of salvation dawned when the Blessed Virgin gave birth to your Son...'. A similar message can be found in a well known passage from Micah 5 (also used in Advent) which follows. Bethlehem, 'the least of the clans of Judah', is invoked; from it will come 'the one who is to rule over Israel' and he will be born of the one who is 'waiting to give birth'. In the Hebrew Bible, the passage is about a restoration of Israel: the 'ruler' will be peace, will bring peace. In the New Testament, it is regarded as referring to Christ who was born at Bethlehem (Mt 2:4-6). The 'ruler' who is born is the Saviour and his mother will be Mary of

Nazareth. The alleluia verse sings of Mary who brings into the world 'the sun of justice', Jesus Christ. In the gospel that follows we are faced with a genealogy, the genealogy of Joseph in fact, with its many and sometimes unidentifiable names. Some find this text difficult. Genealogies were important in Hebrew culture; they established the *legal* paternity of a son, in this case Joseph, 'the supposed father of Jesus', as Luke puts it. In the eyes of the law, then, he was the father of Jesus and, to quote Micah, 'his origin goes back to a distant past'. He is of the Davidic line. Matthew indeed traces the descent from Abraham through Jesse, the father of David, and then (with the omission of some) from the other Davidic kings until the exile. The line is continued until we come to Nathan, 'the father of Joseph, the husband of Mary' *of whom* was born 'Jesus who is called Christ'. Liturgically speaking, this is the most important sentence of the reading. Jesus is the son of Mary, for the 'of whom' applies to Mary alone.

If the genealogy gospel is regarded as pastorally inappropriate, Matthew 1:18-2 may be read. After giving the story of Joseph's doubts and dreams (dispelled by the message from God), it ends with the resounding proclamation from Isaiah: 'The Virgin will conceive and give birth to a son and they will call him Emmanuel, a name that means "God-is-with-us"'. The feast is thus a celebration of Mary *Theotokos* who brought the Saviour into the world. It is for this that she is honoured on this day.

The same line of thought is found in the Office of Readings where the scripture reading is, somewhat surprisingly, Genesis 3:9-20, the account of the Fall and its consequences. There is no need to rehearse the story here. For the liturgy, the most important sentence is the following: 'I will make you enemies of each other: you and the woman, your offspring and her offspring. It will crush your head and you will strike its heel.' The text is foretelling the opposition of the Adversary (the power of evil) to the woman and her 'seed'. In some unknown future the 'seed', the descendant of the woman, will crush the power of the Adversary. In the tradition of the church in the east and the west this text, sometimes called the *Proto-evangelium* (an anticipation of the *gospel*), has been seen as a prophecy of the conflict between the Saviour (the seed of the woman) and the Adversary. Thus it takes up the last sentence of the Matthew passage: Jesus is to be so called 'for he is the Saviour of his people'.

In the Office of Readings of the day, there are other texts that in their own way deliver the same message, as for instance: 'Today, the Virgin Mary was born of the race of David; through her the salvation of the world was made manifest…'. The phrase 'born of the race of David' is, as it were, continued in the short reading of Evening Prayer II. St Paul is writing to the Romans (9:1-5) and speaking of the Jews who, he prays, will ultimately respond to the Christ-Messiah who 'according to the flesh' was one of them. He was descended from the ancient people of God, who had made them his sons and daughters; they had experienced his presence on Sinai and in the Temple; to them were made the promises (of a Messiah) through the centuries but now these promises were fulfilled, and more than fulfilled, in the coming of that Messiah who is the new covenant, the new temple, now present to his new people as he will be until the end of time. The presence of the Lord is now physically manifested by his taking flesh in the womb of the Virgin Mary, a presence that is perpetuated in the sacramental liturgy of the church. Thereby the Lord Jesus can be, and is, present to us as we are to him, in a way that was unknown before he came.

Much of the meaning of the feast is summed up in the homily of St Andrew of Crete (+740) which is appointed for the Office of Readings. He speaks first of the harmonisation of the law and love: Christ transforms the letter into the spirit, he has made law subject to love. This, he continues, is a summary of the benefits Christ has bestowed on us, it is the 'unveiling of the Mystery' whereby nature is renewed, 'God and man, and the deification of the human nature assumed by God'. But so great and glorious a visitation needed a prelude: 'The present feast is such: the prelude is the birth of the mother of God, and the concluding act is the union which is destined between the Word and human nature. A virgin is now born and suckled and moulded and is made ready to be the mother of God, (who is) the king of all for ever.'[2]

This is the mystery we celebrate which brings a twofold gain: we shall be led away from the slavery of the law towards the truth. Grace introduces freedom in place of the letter of the law (cf. 2 Cor 3:17) and the shadow of reality yields to its presence: 'The present feast stands on the border between these. It joins us to the truth instead of signs and figures (of the Old Testament) and brings in the new in place of the old'.

He concludes with an exhortation to rejoice on this feast day: 'For today a shrine is built for the Creator of the universe. The creature (Mary) is made ready as a divine dwelling of the Creator' (*Divine Office*, III, pp. 237-8*).

It is in this way that a writer of the eastern church can teach us the meaning of the feast without ever using the legendary material concerning Mary's parents, though Joachim and Anne are frequently mentioned in the Office of the Byzantine rite of the day. In the birth of Mary Andrew sees the beginning, the prelude of the incarnation of our Lord Jesus Christ who is the Son of God, and Mary can be rightly called *Theotokos*.

Notes

1. See Adolf Adam, *The Liturgical Year* (Pueblo, NY, 1981), p. 217.
2. *Divine Office*, iii, 237*.

CHAPTER 9

The Immaculate Conception of the Blessed Virgin Mary

Solemnity, 8 December

The origins of this feast are obscure and far to seek. Like the dogma, not defined until 1854, it was slow to develop and its object and content remained uncertain. There was a feast of the Conception of Mary long before there was a feast of the Immaculate Conception.

The first mention of the feast about 700 AD in the eastern part of the church, occasioned, it seems, by a certain reading of the second century *Proto-Evangelium* of James, an apocryphal gospel which had been circulating in the east. The feast was centred upon the conception by St Anne of Mary. In the centuries that followed, many Byzantine preachers spoke with great enthusiasm of St Mary and proclaimed her purity. Andrew of Crete (+740) speaks of her as 'the perfect reproduction of the original beauty of mankind' and as 'the only one who is blameless'. Before him Epiphanius (+403) used the word 'undefiled', and *'achrantos'* (undefiled) is found in the eucharistic prayers of John Chrysostom, Basil and James. But the precise theological significance of these terms remained undefined.[1] The same must be said of what seems to be the first feast of which there is record in the so-called Naples Marble Calendar and the *Typica* (also a calendar) of the Greek monasteries of southern Italy in the tenth century. Then, what seems strange, we find that a feast of the Conception of Mary was celebrated in *England* a little later in the eleventh century, about 1020. This continued to be kept until the Conquest when the Normans rather contemptuously abolished it. It was a mere Anglo-Saxon devotion. Its revival by 1140 is associated with the names of Anselm, nephew of the saint, and Eadmer, a monk of Canterbury. He was the first, it seems, to defend an Immaculate Conception of Mary, as he did in his *Tractatus de Conceptione S. Mariae*.[2]

Nonetheless, controversy continued and the great theologians of the Scholastic era debated the matter with vigour. St Thomas Aquinas insisted that Mary *needed* to be redeemed (the *debitum redemptionis*) as, according to the scriptures, every human being did. But Duns Scotus, a Scotsman, produced the thesis that Mary was redeemed by anticipation, by 'the foreseen merits of her son, Jesus Christ', as the definition of 1854 had it. The conclusions of these two theologians left the way open for the establishment of the feast. This a Franciscan Pope, Sixtus IV, did in 1476 for the calendar of the church in Rome. It was extended to the whole church of the Roman rite by Clement XI in 1708. It was not, however, until after the definition of 1854 that the feast appeared under the title of the Immaculate Conception of the Blessed Virgin Mary.

Sixtus IV commissioned one Nogaroli to draw up a Mass (and Office) for the feast which was clear on the Immaculate Conception; the collect 'states the nature and foundation of Mary's privilege' and is said to have inspired the Bull *Ineffabilis* of Pius IX.[3] In 1863 the same Pope commissioned another Mass, the text of which is practically identical with that of Nogaroli.

As it stood in the Roman Missal before 1970, there was the entrance chant, *Gaudens gaudebo*, 'I will rejoice greatly in the Lord!...', the collect, the epistle, drawn from the Wisdom Literature (Prov 8:22-35), once much used for feasts of our Lady, the gradual based in Judith 13, 'Blessed are you, Virgin Mary, above all women on earth' and the alleluia verse was *Tota pulchra es, Maria*, 'Thou art all beautiful, Mary, and original sin is not in you'. For votive Masses when the Alleluia was suppressed, Psalms 86, 'Glorious things are told of you, City of God', was laid under contribution for the Tract. The gospel was very short, Luke 1:26-28, ending however with the well known words, *Ave Maria, gratia plena...*' which was regarded as a proof text for the dogma or at least an argument from tradition. There was no special Preface. The collect, bearing the marks of Nogaroli's text of the fifteenth century, has been preserved in the formulary of the 1970 missal: 'Lord God, by the Immaculate Conception of the Virgin Mary you prepared a worthy dwelling for your Son and by foreseeing his death you preserved her from all stain (of sin);

grant that by her intercession we too may come to you free from sin'. (In the prayer over the offerings we find the phrase *'gratia praeveniente'*, the grace that 'went before', in this case that anticipated the saving work of Jesus Christ in time).

In the missal as it is now, the Mass formulary is that of the revision: two readings before the gospel divided by a psalm and alleluia verse. Then there is the gospel, now extended to include the whole of the annunciation story. When, however, we consider the texts, especially the reading from Genesis (3:9-15, 20) and that from Ephesians (1:3-6, 11, 12), we see that it is the role of Mary in the history of salvation that is emphasised. She is the mother of the Saviour and that can be dimly discerned in Genesis, which is so difficult to interpret. The scene is the Fall, or rather what happened after the Fall. In mythical terms, deriving from an ancient tradition, the author sees that sin entered the world through the failure of Adam and Eve to resist the temptation to make themselves 'like gods'. They had severed themselves from friendship with God and the consequences are drawn out. The serpent is the symbol of evil, and in terms of primitive natural history, its slithering along in the dust of the earth is seen as its permanent condemnation. It will, however, continue to be the enemy of the human race until in some distant future its power will be crushed by the offspring (the seed) of the woman who will be the 'mother of the living' in a way that Eve could never be. It is the 'seed' who will do the crushing and he will be born of the woman. Mary is the second Eve – that is an ancient theme of the Fathers of the church and is found as early as Irenaeus (c. 200): 'Eve, by her disobedience, brought death upon herself and the human race: Mary, by her obedience, brought salvation'.[4] She brought forth the one who is Saviour of the world and is called *Janua caeli*. Newman, commenting on this title of the Litany of Loreto, says: 'Mary is called the Gate of Heaven, because it was through her that our Lord passed from heaven to earth... (in this way) she had a place in the economy of redemption;... it was fitting then that in God's mercy, that as the woman began the destruction of the world, so woman should also begin its recovery... Mary opened the way for the great achievement of the second Adam, even Our Lord Jesus Christ, who came to save the world by dying on the cross for it'.[5]

The theme is continued in the second reading in a different and very profound way. The text speaks of the 'destiny' of those who are to be redeemed by Jesus Christ. There are in fact two words used here: God *chose us* in Christ and *destined* us (RSV trans.) to be holy and spotless, his holy people, his adopted children in Christ. The text invites us to contemplate the mysterious 'purpose' of God who in eternity 'foresaw' (words are difficult here) his plan of salvation (cf. verse 9) which would culminate in the redeeming word and work of his beloved Son. The liturgical text (used on several feasts of Our Lady in the *Divine Office*) suggests that in the foreseeing or determining of the coming of the Son into this world Mary was included. She was specially 'chosen' to be his mother, specially chosen to be 'holy and spotless' by 're-demption through his blood' (verse 7, omitted in the liturgical passage). The sending of the Son was not an 'after-thought' and before all time Mary was to have her part in bringing into the world the Saviour of the human race. For this reason, she was to be holy and spotless, *amómos*, a word that is used of the church in 5:27. In a word, the destiny of Mary was involved in the destiny of her son. That is what the church through the liturgy is saying on this day. In this perspective, the text comes close to the 'foreseen merits of Christ' of the definition of the dogma.

The psalm continues the theme of salvation of which Mary was the first beneficiary and, as so many patristic and liturgical texts say, she brought forth the *Saviour*: 'All the ends of the earth have seen the salvation of our God.' The infancy gospel of St Luke is best seen as a theological statement (1:26-38), a theological statement about Mary's role in salvation history and about the nature of her condition. Chosen from before all ages, we now see that she is 'highly favoured', she is fully 'engraced' (a similar word is used in Ephesians 1:6: the 'grace he (God) freely bestowed on us in the Beloved'), the Lord (Yahweh) is with her, his 'favour' is with her so that she could become the mother of the Holy Child who 'will be called' and is 'the Son of God'. The efficacious sign of her engraced condition and of her motherhood is the coming upon her of the Holy Spirit who is the power of the Most High. She is henceforth the dwelling place of the Davidic king (*Turris Davidica*), the Tabernacle of the Son of the Most High, or again in a title of the Litany of Loreto, the House of God. By the power of the Holy Spirit she is *Mater Salvatoris*, the mother of Jesus 'who will save his people from their sins' (Mt 1:21).

Much of this is encapsulated in phrases of the Preface of the Mass: 'Full of grace, she was to be a worthy mother of your Son... Purest of Virgins, she was to bring forth your Son, the innocent Lamb who takes away the sin of the world.' It is for this we praise her, for this we thank God for her and all he has done for her.

Reflecting on the title of the feast, one begins to see that its meaning goes far beyond mere 'preservation' from sin. 'Immaculate', 'unstained', 'unblemished' are all negative terms. If we turn once again to the gospel all is positive: 'Joyful greetings to you... Hail, favoured one of God... The Lord is with you.' If the Lord is with Mary, if she is the favoured one, that means that God has given her a great gift, the gift we call grace. She was so filled with grace that she never experienced the alienation we call sin. Or, to put the matter in another way, God's grace so filled her being that she was established in that right relationship with God that we call salvation. The feast of the Immaculate Conception is a celebration of God's love poured into the soul of Mary by the Holy Spirit: 'The Holy Spirit will come upon you and the power of the Most High will overshadow you' and she will be the Mother of God.

Notes

1. For the foregoing see *Catholic Dictionary of Theology*, II, s.v. Conception, Blessed Virgin Mary, p. 74 (Thomas Nelson, London, 1967).

2. *Op. cit.* p. 76. The whole article runs from p. 71 to p. 80 and was written by E. O'Connor, OFM. See also Edmund Bishop, *Liturgica Historica* (Oxford University Press, 1918) 'On the Origins of the Feast of the Conception of the Blessed Virgin Mary', pp. 257, 258.

3. See *The Church at Prayer*, IV ed. A. G. Martimort (London, 1985), p. 140.

4. Irenaeus, *Adversus Haereses*, III, 22, 4 (ET, H. B. Bettenson, *The Early Christian* Writers, 1956, p. 101).

5. See John Henry Newman, *Mediations and Devotions* (London, 1953/1960), pp. 35-6.

CHAPTER 10

The Blessed Virgin Mary in Advent

In the Spanish (Mozarabic) liturgy of centuries ago, there was a feast of the Expectation of St Mary which was observed on 18 December. The church was with Mary who was awaiting the birth of her son, Jesus, and it could be said to sum up the mood of much of Advent, but especially that part of it that runs from 17 to 24 December, when the liturgical texts speak again and again of the role of Mary in the incarnation and birth of the Son of God. In the former Roman Missal, in use up to 1970, the third week was dominated by Marian texts. On Wednesday, the first reading was from Isaiah 7:10-15 (The Virgin will conceive... Emmanuel) and the gospel was Luke 1:26-38, the Annunciation to Mary. On this gospel St Bernard preached his sermons called the *Missus est*, the first words of that gospel passage; they became very famous and were often quoted. On Friday, the first reading was Isaiah 11:1-5, *Egredietur flos de radice Jesse* (A flower will come forth from the root of Jesse), liturgically and traditionally applied to Mary. The gospel was Luke 1:39-47, the Visitation. There were other Marian texts too such as the *Ave Maria, gratia plena, Dominus tecum, benedicta tu in mulieribus*, sung as an offertory antiphon. In the Roman Missal of 1970, these and other texts are distributed over the last Sunday of Advent and the days during the week from 17 to 23. With one or two exceptions, these texts have been commented upon elsewhere in this book but it will be useful to the reader to list them here. They give a clear insight into the role of Mary in the Advent liturgy. For the Fourth Sunday of Advent in the years A, B, C, the following are the readings respectively:

Isaiah 7:10-15, gospel, Matthew 1:18-24 (the annunciation to Joseph).

1 Samuel 7:1-16 (the promise that the throne would never pass
from the house of David (cf. Lk 1:32).
Micah 5:1-4 (refs. to Bethlehem, to 'her who is to give birth' and
to the Messiah).
Luke 1:39-44, the Visitation.
The days 17-24 December have a considerable number of texts
some of which however are duplicates of those found on the
Sundays:
17 December: Genesis 49:2-10 (The sceptre shall not pass from
          Judah),
          Matthew 1:1-17 (the genealogy)
18 December: Jeremiah 23:5-8 (virtuous branch of David)
          Matthew 1:18-24 (The Virgin will conceive...
          Emmanuel)
19 December: Judges 13:2-7, 24, 25 (Samson the nazirite)
          Luke 1:5-25 (annunciation of John the Baptist)
20 December: Isaiah 7:10-14
          Luke 1:26-38 (annunciation to Mary)
21 December: Song of Songs 2:18-14 (the call of the lover) or
          Zephaniah 3:14-18; (daughter of Zion... the king is in
          your midst)
          Luke 1:39-45 (the visitation)
22 December: 1 Samuel 1:24-28 (dedication of Hannah's only
          son), (Song of Hannah: 2:4-8)
          Luke 1:46-56 (the Magnificat)
23 December: Malachi 3:1-4, 23, 24 (the messenger to prepare the
          way)
          Luke 1:57-66 (birth of John the Baptist)
24 December: 1 Samuel 7:1-5 etc (as above for Advent B)
          Luke 1:67-79 (*Benedictus*)

It will be seen that, with certain Messianic texts from the Old
Testament, there are grouped on these days all the passages of
the infancy gospels that refer to the conception and imminent
birth of Christ. Jeremiah 23, Judges in its own way, and 1 Samuel
in its way, are foreshadowings of the Messiah, as is Genesis 49.
Combined with the story of Mary is that of John the Baptist, the
forerunner of Jesus. In these ways, the history of salvation and
Mary's position is suggested by these texts. She is inseparably

bound up with the prophecies of the Messiah, with the conception and birth and future mission of the Baptist, and she has a central place in the proclamation of the coming, conception and birth of the Son of God which are announced in these texts. As has been said, most of these texts have received some commentary in the feasts where they occur. It remains to say a few words about those texts that appear for the first time.

The chapter in which the verse about Judah occurs looks both to the past (the work of the patriarchs) and to the future. It is to be regarded as prophetic and, according to the experts, the whole chapter in its present form was inserted into the bible in the time of King David. In this sense, it is Messianic, referring to the house of David from which will come the Messiah. There are hints of this in the words, 'The sceptre shall not pass from Judah' and the one that holds it is a sign of hope. In the verse, 11, that follows, there are somewhat obscure references to the Messiah: He tethers his donkey to the vine/to its stock the foal of the she-donkey (cf. Zechariah 9:9). Of the house of David came Joseph and it is usually supposed that Mary did too, as people married within the clan (See *NJB*, 49:10, n.a). Jeremiah 23 is clearly Messianic. The prophet is speaking of the restoration of Israel, Yahweh will bring back the 'remnant' from captivity and will raise up 'Branch' (which became a Messianic proper name) and in his days 'Judah will triumph' and he will be called 'Yahweh-is-our-saving-justice' (See *NJB*, notes a and b). The 'Branch' will come from Mary and he will bring salvation. The Book of Judges may seem a far cry from the New Testament, but in the passage referred to above, the church has seen Samson as a 'type' of the Messiah. Samson is born thanks to a divine intervention: 'A man of God has just come to me: his presence was like the presence of the angel of God', and he says to the wife of Manoah, 'You will conceive and bear a son' who will be a nazirite abstaining from strong drink and anything unclean. The parallels with the annunciation gospel are obvious, as are the differences, but the passage seems to have been introduced for the play on the words 'nazirite' and Nazareth. Or perhaps we can say that it is the story of a miraculous birth which has some similarity to the account in Luke.

In 1 Samuel 1, Hannah, a childless wife, at the prayer of the priest Eli, gives birth to a son, her only son, who is called Samuel and, as she had promised, she brings him to the temple to dedicate him to the service there and to the worship of God. She then utters her prayer of thanksgiving which, it has long been remarked, has certain similarities to the Magnificat that forms the gospel of the day. It has been called a model upon which the Magnificat was based or which influenced its composition. It is interesting to note that it is a song of the 'poor ones' (the *anawim*): 'The bows of the mighty are broken/but the weak are clothed with strength' and, 'he lifts up the lowly from the dust/from the dung-heap he raises the poor' (cf. Ps 112). This is interesting because Mary is among the *anawim* who with Joseph, Simeon and others were 'looking for the redemption of Israel'. But the Magnificat has a depth of feeling that is lacking in the song of Hannah: 'My soul proclaims the greatness of the Lord/ and my spirit exults in God my Saviour.../ he has looked on his lowly handmaid.../ he has done great things for me and holy is his name.' The next verses, about putting down the mighty and exalting the lowly and feeding the hungry, are very much the prayer of the *anawim*. Then in the last verses there is recalling of salvation history with its mention of Israel and Abraham and his progeny who will be saved by the redeeming work of Jesus, the Son of God who is also the son of Mary. As is evident, the readings of 23 and 24 December concern John the Baptist and thus complete the whole cycle of readings appointed for these days.

Reviewing what might be called this special lectionary, we can see that it assembles almost every text of the Old and New Testaments that can be said to have relevance to Mary and her place in salvation history.

The liturgical texts of the season, of course, reflect the scriptures and in different ways draw out their meaning. For the Fourth Sunday there is the well known prayer that concludes the Angelus. We pray that the Lord will pour his grace into our hearts so that we who, through the message of an angel have come to know the incarnation of Christ, the Son of God, may through his passion and cross may be brought to the glory of his resurrection. It is a comprehensive prayer, setting out the whole process of salvation history as brought about by the birth, passion, death and resurrection of Jesus Christ.

In the days from 17 to 23 December the special collects exploit the teaching of the gospels. God's loving plan of salvation was that the Word should take flesh (Jn 1:14) in the womb of the Virgin Mary (Lk 1:35), and we pray that through him, the Son of God, who shared our human nature, we may share his divine nature (2 Pet 1:4). On the 19 December we are reminded that the child born to Mary is the revelation of the splendour of the divine glory (Heb 1:3), and we are incited to celebrate with faith and reverence the mystery of the incarnation. The collect for 20 December recalls the annunciation: the angel announces, Mary is filled with light, and gives her consent (Lk 1:38), and we pray that, like her, we may accept God's will and do it. Finally, the prayer for 23 December refers to the incarnation: the Word takes flesh in the womb of the Blessed Virgin Mary and comes to dwell among us (Jn 1:14).

If we think of Advent in the terms of the Expectation of Mary, the second Preface for the season has a moving passage. It recalls Christ's coming foretold by the prophets and by John the Baptist 'who made him known when at last he came', and then speaks of Mary, 'the virgin mother (who) bore him in her womb *with love beyond all telling*'. That, it seems to me, says it all.

According to the Roman Calendar of 1969, Advent has two themes, the eschatological concerning the end-time, and preparation for the celebration of Christmas. In the Missal and the Lectionary the first is the main and exclusive theme in the first weeks; in the *Divine Office* the second is anticipated, with the result that from 1 Advent the office has a distinctly Marian flavour. Thus on the First Sunday of Advent for Evening Prayer 1 we find as an antiphon an evocation of Luke 1:35: 'The Holy Spirit will come upon you and you will bear in your womb the Son of God.' The antiphons for the Day Hours on Sundays and week days are all from Luke 1. Sunday Advent II evokes Luke 1:45, 'Blessed are you because you had faith...', and Monday (second week) paraphrases Luke 1:35: 'The angel of the Lord brought good news to Mary and she conceived by the power of the Holy Spirit'. In antiphon 3 the Magnificat is quoted: 'All generations will call me blessed, for God has looked upon his lowly handmaid.' On Thursday Evening, we have 'Before they came together Mary was found with child through the Holy Spirit' (Mt 1:20). These antiphons, with the prayers and scripture texts mentioned above, help us to reflect on the role of Mary in salvation history and during the celebration of the liturgy in Advent.

Among the patristic readings for the Office of Readings there are a few passages that carry forward the themes of Advent concerning the Blessed Virgin. St Gregory of Nazianzen emphasises the purity of Mary who was both mother and virgin: 'He took to himself all that is human, except sin. He was conceived by the Virgin who was first purified in body and soul by the Spirit. It was necessary both that childbearing be honoured and that virginity be honoured still more highly' (Orat. 45; *Divine Office* 1: p. 58). Commenting on Genesis 3, Irenaeus draws out the parallels and differences in Eve and Mary: 'Just as Eve, seduced by an angel's message (i.e. Satan), turned away from God in betraying his word, so Mary, welcoming an angel's message, bore God within her in obeying his word. Eve had been led to disobey God, but Mary consented to obey him, and so the Virgin Mary became the advocate of the virgin Eve.' Lower down he contrasts Jesus with Adam: 'From that time he who was to be born of the woman, the Virgin, in the likeness of Adam was announced as "watching for the head" of the serpent.' Adam and the Second Adam, Christ, Eve and the second Eve, Mary, are constantly in the mind of Irenaeus as he ponders on the mystery of the incarnation (*Adv. Haereses* V, 19: *D.V.* 1 p. 92). The Cistercian writer, Isaac of Stella, exploits the theme: Christ, head and body (the church) and Mary, the mother of the church: 'For Christ, head and body, is one, whole and unique; but this one Christ is of one God in heaven and one mother on earth; this Christ is both many sons and one. For as head and body are one son and many sons, so Mary and the church are one mother and many; one virgin and many' (Sermon 52; *D.V.* 1 p. 95). For 20 December we have one of St Bernard's famous sermons (4) on the annunciation and Mary's consent. We are waiting for her consent, the world 'overwhelmed by wretchedness' awaits her consent: 'In the eternal Word were we all made and lo! we die; by one little word of yours in answer shall we be made alive.' Then he, as it were, dramatises the situation: 'Open your heart to faith; open your lips to speak… the Desired of the nations is outside… Arise by faith, run by the devotion of your heart, open by your word. And Mary said: Behold the handmaid of the Lord: be it done to me according to your word.' For the Visitation gospel (21 December) St Ambrose supplies the commentary from which we extract the following exhortation: 'Let the soul of Mary be in each one of you to magnify the Lord. Let the spirit of Mary be in each one of you to exult in God. According to the flesh, one woman is the mother of Christ, but according to faith, Christ is the fruit of all. Every soul, indeed, receives the Word of God, provided it remains unstained and free from sin and preserves its chastity in unviolated modesty' (Comment on Luke, Bk 2; *D.V.* 1: pp. 149-150).

Finally, we have St Bede the Venerable as the commentator on the Magnificat for 22 December. Bede's sober piety comes through: 'The Lord, she said, has exalted me with a great and unheard of gift, which cannot be explained in any words and can scarcely be understood by the deepest feelings of the heart. And so I offer up all the strength of my soul in thanksgiving and praise. In my joy I pour out all my life, all my feelings, all my understanding in contemplation of the greatness of him who is without end. My spirit rejoices in the eternal divinity of Jesus, my Saviour, whom I have conceived in time and bear in my body' (Comment on Luke, Bk 1; *D.V.* 1. p. 156).

These and other commentaries on the scriptures, along with the liturgical texts, help us to see the *Divine Office* not so much as many words but as a means of contemplation on the great and life-giving mysteries of the faith.

CHAPTER 11

Our Lady of Sorrows

Memoria, 15 September

As has been suggested above, development of devotion to our Lady has been a long one. It is discernible in the middle of the third century, it developed rapidly after the Council of Ephesus (431), especially in the eastern churches, and, as we have seen, in the west in the seventh century. After that there was a pause. Circumstances in the west were not at all propitious for theological development or any kind of development. In the eleventh century, things began to change, human living became a little easier, prosperity began to increase, and recognisable 'nations' began to appear. At the same time, there seems to have been a change of religious psychology, new needs began to appear and gradually this became apparent in devotional life. Various factors were in play and one of them was a change in attitude towards Christ. Devotion became more personal. For centuries in both the east and the west, in apses and mosaics Christ was depicted as *Christus Pantocrator*, the Ruler of the Universe. Even the cross portrayed him as reigning from the tree: *Regnavit a ligno Deus*: God has reigned from the cross. There was also the *crux gemmata*, the jewelled cross, on which was no figure of the Lord, and there was no crucifix on the altar until about the eleventh century. As for Mary, there were the great and still moving frescoes, dominating the altar and sanctuary, of the woman, usually holding the child before her, which seem to suggest as much the mother of the church as the mother of Christ.

Although there are traces of a personal and felt relationship with Christ in the seventh century, it was not until the eleventh century that emphasis on the humanity of Christ began to appear. It has been said that 'Devotion to the humanity of Christ was the great medieval innovation'.[1] It seems to have had as its point of departure a closer attention to the gospel narratives of the birth of Christ and those concerning the passion. The sermons of St Bernard are a well known and eloquent testimony of this. Indeed, it could be said that the Cistercian Order was the great exponent and promoter of this form of devotion which gradually found its way into the liturgy. From the thirteenth century onwards Franciscans and others followed the Cistercians.

Since Mary was so deeply concerned with the events of the incarnation, and since St John represents her as standing at the foot of the cross, she too became in a new way a centre of interest. So we get paintings of Mary, the mother of Jesus, at Bethlehem and, from about the fourteenth century, pictures of her holding her son after he had been taken down from the cross (the Pietà). Then later still celebrations in the liturgy.

It was in this atmosphere that a celebrationof the Sorrows of our Lady was kept in Germany in 1423. It, however, remained a local celebration for several centuries, until Pope Benedict XIII inserted into the calendar a feast of 'The Seven Sorrows of the Blessed Virgin Mary' in 1721. It was to be observed on the Friday before Palm Sunday, thus indicating its connection with the passion of our Lord. Pius X, in 1913, wishing to preserve the days of Lent intact, moved it to 15 September (the day after the Exaltation of the Cross) where it still remains. In the revision of the liturgy after the Second Vatican Council, the Mass and the Office of the day have received new formularies. The thirteenth century hymn, *Stabat Mater* (now attributed to Saint Bonaventure), has been retained as a sequence after the first reading of the Mass though its use is optional. In fact it does not fit very well into the liturgy of the word; it is too long, and as the feast now occurs only on a weekday, it cannot be sung in almost all churches.

The revision of the texts of the day is very much in line with the teaching of chapter 8 of the *Constitution on the Church* and the *Marialis Cultus* of Paul VI. In the Mass, then, we have as the first reading Hebrews 5:7-9, a picture of Jesus Christ 'offering prayer and entreaty' during his lifetime but especially in Gethsemane 'aloud and in silent tears' and submitting totally and with loving obedience to his father. He was 'saved' by the father, for his death was transformed by the resurrection so that he was 'perfected' in his role as priest and victim. By consequence, he could become for all who obey him 'the source of eternal salvation'. The psalms that follows (30:2-6, 15-16, 20) is used in the liturgy of Good Friday (though with different verses) and echoes the words of Jesus as he was dying:

> Release me from the snares they have hidden
> for you are my refuge, Lord.
> Into your hands I commend my spirit,
> It is you who will redeem me, Lord (cf. Lk 23:46).

The association of Mary with the dying Saviour is proclaimed in the gospel of the day: 'Near the cross of Jesus stood his mother…' (Jn 19:25-27). This is unique to John's gospel and, though for this celebration, the emphasis is on the com-passion of Mary with her son, there may be the suggestion of something deeper, a theological mystery. In Jesus' words 'Woman, this is your son' and 'this is your mother,' we can discern that Mary is being established as mother of the church, the church that is the body of Christ extended in space and time, the church that suffers and has suffered throughout the ages both from attacks from enemies without and defections from within. That same church is also called to imitate Mary in suffering for the church and seeking her help.[2]

The alternative gospel (Lk 2:33-35) yields a similar message. Jesus, in the first weeks after his birth, is already a sign that will be contradicted, and Mary, the daughter of Zion, is involved in the destiny of her own people. She will be at the centre of the contradiction when 'the secret thoughts of many will be laid bare', for or against her son, and the 'sword' of division will pierce her heart as the lance will pierce the heart of her son. (Jn 19:37 and cf. Zech 12:10).[3]

The Opening Prayer of the Mass (also used in the *Divine Office*) combines these two thoughts:

> 'God our Father, as your son was raised on the cross,
> his mother Mary stood by him, sharing his sufferings.

May your church be united with Christ in his suffering
and death
and so come to share in his rising to new life....

The antiphon to the *Benedictus* reflects the emphasis on the resurrection through which Mary is in glory: 'Rejoice, grief-stricken
Mother, for you share the triumph of your Son...'. On the other
hand, the redeeming work of Jesus is highlighted in antiphon 3,
Evening Prayer, and we are reminded that, like Mary, we are to
share in his sufferings: 'As sharers in Christ's sufferings, let us
rejoice' (Morning Prayer, antiphon 2). The Short Reading speaks
of the sufferings of the church, the body of Christ, which we
share by working for it, as St Paul did (Col 1:24, 25). Christ,
Mary, the church and ourselves are all brought together here.

What may seem surprising is that Mary is said to have won the
crown of martyrdom though without suffering the pain of death
(Versicle, Evening Prayer). This seems to be prompted by a
statement in the homily of St Bernard (Office of Readings): 'Do
not marvel that Mary is said to have endured martyrdom in her
soul.' This is preceded at the beginning of the homily with some
words that became well known: 'Blessed Mother, a sword did
pierce your soul. For no sword could pierce your son's flesh
without piercing your soul. After your own son Jesus gave up
his life... the cruel lance, which opened his side... could not
touch his soul. But it pierced your soul... and (your soul) was
pierced by a sword of sorrow. We rightly speak of you as more
than martyr, for the anguish of mind you suffered exceeded all
bodily pain.'[4]

A martyr is a witness to Christ and to his word, and Bernard
evidently saw Mary as witness to her son, the word made flesh,
and she suffered with him at the cross and so became a witness
to his sufferings and a sharer in them.

Reviewing all the liturgical texts of the day one finds that it is a
very balanced message about the deeper meaning of the Sorrows
of Mary. It is no longer a presentation of purely subjective suffering on her part but an invitation to enter into a deeper union
with the suffering Christ, and with Mary who at the cross en-

tered more deeply into that suffering than any other human being. We may conclude with St Bernard: 'Charity it was that moved him to suffer death, charity greater than that of any man before or since: charity too moved Mary, the like of which no mother has ever known.'[5]

Notes

1. See J. A. Jungmann, SJ, *Pastoral Liturgy* (ET, London, 1962), p. 56 and the whole section 7, pp. 48-58.

2. For 'Woman' see Raymond E. Brown, *The Gospel according to John*, Vol. 2, p. 926 (The Anchor Bible, Geoffrey Chapman, London, 1966-1982-1984). He thinks that the title 'Woman', recalling 'Eve' of the Book of Genesis, suggests the 'New Eve'.

3. See the *New Jerusalem Bible*, (London, 1985), notes 1 and m on verse 38.

4. As in *Divine Office*, III, p. 265.*

5. ibid p. 263* and for end of homily p. 263.*

CHAPTER 12

The Presentation of the Blessed Virgin Mary

Memoria, 21 November

It may seem strange that this memoria, which may be based on a legend in the apocryphal gospel of St James (referred to in a previous chapter), should be included in the official calendar of the church of the Roman rite. It was in fact excluded by Pius V (+1572) and put back by one of the successors, a Franciscan Pope, Sixtus V, in 1585. It was retained by the Roman Calendar of 1969 no doubt because of its ecumenical relevance. It is a feast in the calendar of the Orthodox Church and it was in fact in the east where the celebration originated.

Whether or not affected by the legend, the celebration was originally a feast of the dedication of a church of Saint Mary in Jerusalem on 21 November 543. It is then connected with the establishment of the first feast of St Mary (see chapter 2). A feast under the title of the Presentation was kept in Constantinople in the eighth century and made its way west like other Marian feasts. In the eleventh century, it is mentioned in the Greek calendar (the *Typica*) which, as we have seen, also refers to a feast of the Conception of Mary. From there it was brought to England in the twelfth century, and was celebrated in the papal chapel at Avignon in the fourteenth century. As indicated above, it has been in the Roman Calendar since 1585.

The texts are from the Common of the Blessed Virgin Mary but otherwise are very reserved about any use of the temple theme. The first reading of the Mass suggested by the Lectionary is Zechariah 2:14-17 that refers to the 'daughter of Zion', Mary, and speaks of the Lord coming to dwell in her and making Jerusalem his very own. The gospel is Matthew 12:46-50, about doing the will of God. The responsorial psalm is the whole of the Magnificat. The collect of Mass and Office is quite general. The antiphon of the Magnificat at Second Evening Prayer speaks of Mary as 'the temple of the Lord, the sacred dwelling-place of the Holy Spirit', thus transforming the physical building into the spiritual temple, the abode of the Holy Spirit (cf. Lk 1:35).

The Patristic reading of the Office, from a sermon of St Augustine, has several bold statements that give rise to reflection. She was 'by Christ created that Christ in her might be created... She did the Father's will... and it is a greater thing for her that she was Christ's disciple than that she was his mother'. Does this somewhat downgrade the importance of the motherhood? Commenting further on 'Blessed rather those who hear the word of God and keep it', he says: 'Her mind was filled more fully with the truth than her womb by the flesh. Christ is the truth, God is made flesh: Christ the truth is in Mary's mind, Christ made flesh is in her womb. Greater is that which is in her mind than that which she carries in her womb.'

He goes on to say, as does the *Constitution on the Church*, that Mary is part of the church: 'She is a holy member of the church... she is the member above all members but she is still a member... and if so, the body is certainly greater than the member....' The Lord is head, we all are members of the body and we shall be the sort of members we ought to be if, like Mary, we do the will of the Father.

CHAPTER 13

Other Celebrations of the
Blessed Virgin Mary

Our Lady of Lourdes
Optional Memoria, 11 February
In 1854 Pope Pius IX declared that the Blessed Virgin Mary was conceived immaculate and that this was now a defined doctrine of the church. In 1858 Mary appeared to Bernadette Soubirous for the first time on 11 February. In the course of subsequent appearances, at the request of Bernadette, the Lady answered that she was the Immaculate Conception. She called for prayer, penitence and charity. By 1860 or so, crowds from different parts of France began to assemble at Lourdes and, as the means of communication improved, people came from all parts of Europe and then from almost every country of the world.

However one may explain it, Lourdes is a phenomenon that has played a large part in the life of the modern church. Pius X instituted a feast on 11 February, 1908, and a Mass and an Office were drawn up under the title of 'The Feast of the Apparitions of the Blessed Virgin Mary'. In the Roman Calendar of 1969 it is called a 'Memorial of Our Lady of Lourdes', to emphasise that it is a celebration of the Blessed Virgin herself. Emphasis on the 'appearances' has been removed. This is expressed very well in the antiphon to the Benedictus: 'Bright dawn of salvation, Virgin Mary; from you rose the Sun of Justice, the Rising Sun, who came to visit us on high' This is a quite classical text showing that Mary is the mother of the Saviour whom she brought into the world.

With the exception of the above and the collect of the Mass and Office, the texts are from the Common of the Blessed Virgin Mary. The Collect neatly summarises the main aspects of the celebration. Recalling Mary, immaculate Mother of God, the church asks that, through her prayer, strength may be given to the weak (whether of soul or body) and for grace to rise up from sin (the penitential side of Lourdes).

The second reading for the Office of Readings is taken from a description Bernadette wrote, while in her convent at Nevers, of the appearances of Our Lady to her when she was a girl of fourteen. Perhaps few will realise what this cost her. When she got to the convent it is improbable that she could write and, in any case, she had to learn 'proper' French as her language at home was the local patois. There was a second difficulty that was much greater. When people tried to draw or paint pictures of the Lady as she appeared, Bernadette rejected them all. None of them was 'like'. When she began to write she was aware of these difficulties. At Nevers, next to the convent chapel, is a small museum where photocopies of Bernadette's writings are exposed. From these we can see how she struggled to write down her experiences. Sometimes she crosses out a word and then another word because they did not express exactly what she wanted to say. Then there is a third word with which she seems to have been satisfied. These are visible signs both of her honesty and of her determination. In addition, she had to fight ill-health. Asked how she was getting on she replied, 'I am getting on with my life.' The questioner then asked 'What is that?' Bernadette answered 'Being ill.' It is good to learn that she was canonised not for her visions 'but for her humble simplicity and her religious trustworthiness'.[1]

The Immaculate Heart of Mary
Obligatory Memoria
Saturday following Second Sunday after Pentecost
This celebration has its origin in the Marian devotion of St John Eudes and his missionary congregation in seventeenth-century France. Rules about instituting feasts in those days were less rigorous than now and he and his followers began keeping a feast of the Sacred Heart of Mary. In the early nineteenth-century this was recognised by Pius VII who fixed the Octave of the Assumption as the day of its celebration. In the pontificate of Pius XII, the appearances of Our Lady at Fatima in 1917 influenced that Pope, it seems, to insert a feast under the title of The

Immaculate Heart of Mary into the Roman Calendar. In 1996 it was made an obligatory memoria.

The Mass and Office are mostly from the Common of the Blessed Virgin Mary. The opening prayer of the Mass refers to the heart of Mary as a fitting dwelling of the Holy Spirit, evidently recalling the gospel saying that the Holy Spirit would come upon Mary.

In the Office of the day there is a reference to 'the temple of the heart', the place of the Lord's dwelling, and the antiphon of the Magnificat for Evening Prayer replaces 'spirit' with 'heart'.

Our Lady of Mount Carmel
Optional Memoria, 16 July
This is an important celebration in the Carmelite calendar. It commemorates the origin of the Carmelite Order on Mount Carmel in the twelfth century. The Rule was drawn up and approved in the thirteenth century. The Order has an interesting English connection. The Englishman, Simon Stock (+1265), had a vision of the Mother of God precisely on this date when he was General of the Order. A feast of this title was introduced in the fourteenth century, which was extended to the calendar of the Roman rite in 1726 but reduced to an optional memoria in 1969.

The liturgical texts are those of the Common of the Blessed Virgin Mary for the most part but some proper to the feast are very apt. Thus the first reading, which may be read at the Mass, Zechariah 2:14-17, refers to the 'daughter of Zion' which in an accommodated sense is applied to Mary and goes on to evoke 'the Holy Land' where the Carmelite Order was born. There is a reference to the contemplative character of the Order in the words, 'Let all mankind be silent before the Lord', and the gospel, Matthew 12:46-50, suggests the same message: 'Anyone who does the will of my Father in heaven, he is my brother, and sister and mother'– which nicely includes the friars and the nuns!

In the collect of the day we find a reference to Mount Carmel: we pray that we may come to the mountain of God, Christ the Lord. The Office of the day is given 'personality' by the antiphon of the Benedictus: 'I sought wisdom openly in my prayers; it has

come to flower like early grapes.' Again, it refers to the fruits of
contemplation of which the early grapes of the Holy Land are
the metaphor. The Office is further enriched by an extract from
the famous first Homily of St Leo for the Nativity of the Lord.
The first paragraph is a commentary on Luke 1:26-36:

'A royal virgin of the race of David is chosen to bear the holy
child whom she conceived in her soul before she conceived him
in her body. And lest she might be afraid when something so
unexpected came to pass, not knowing the divine plan, she was
shown in her conversation with the angel that what was to be ac-
complished in her would be the work of the Holy Spirit; she
would soon be the Mother of God without loss of virginity...
Her trusting faith was confirmed by a miracle already accomp-
lished. Elizabeth was given unhoped-for fertility...' (*Divine
Office*, III, p. 115). Leo continues with his theology of the incarnation in terms very like his great *Tomus* that was decisive at the
Council of Chalcedon (451) several years later.

The Dedication of the Basilica of St Mary Major
Optional Memoria, 5 August
As the title of this memoria shows it really commemorates the
dedication of a church and should more properly be regarded as
a feast of the Lord, as all other church dedications are. But in this
case there are special circumstances. After the definition of Mary
as the *Theotokos*, Mother of God, by the Council of Ephesus (431),
Pope Sixtus III built the church called St Mary Major to com-
memorate the definition of the council and in honour of Mary,
the Mother of God. At first it was a purely Roman celebration
but in about the fourteenth century a legend was circulating that
the ground plan of the church had been outlined in *snow* (!) on 5
August, usually the hottest time of the summer (the *ferragosto*).
This legend was believed and after Rome had been cleaned up
in the sixteenth century (mostly by St Philip Neri), the feast became popular and Pius V inserted it into the Roman Calendar.
The liturgical texts indicate that it is now a celebration of the
motherhood of St Mary: 'Holy Mary, Mother of God, ever-virgin:
you are the most blessed of all women, and blessed is the fruit of
your womb' (antiphon, Benedictus). The homily of the Office of
Readings is an exuberant sermon of St Cyril of Alexander in

praise of the Mother of God. The readings at Mass may be Apocalypse 21:1-5 (used for the dedication of a church) and Luke 11:27, 28: 'Blessed is the womb that bore you... rather blessed are those who hear the word of God and keep it.'

Our Lady, Queen and Mother
Memoria, 22 August

The 1950s were a time of somewhat over-heated devotion to our Lady. The theologians were busy too; there were those who were pressing for definitions: that Mary is the Mediatress of All Graces and that she was Co-Redemptress. These matters were put in proper perspective by the Second Vatican Council with its document, *The Constitution on the Church*, chapter VIII. Pope Pius XII had defined the Assumption of Our Lady as a dogma of the church in 1950 and in 1954 declared a Marian Year. This he concluded with the institution of the Feast of Our Lady, Queen and Mother, to draw out the connection between her role of Queen of heaven and earth with the Assumption.

The church of course had long celebrated Mary as Queen in anthems such as *Regina Caeli* and *Salve Regina* which were and are parts of the Liturgy of the Hours. In the Litany of Loreto, Mary is invoked as Queen many times and there are numerous hymns both ancient and modern that mention her as Queen. The Pope's intention, however, was to show that the Assumption is the exaltation of Mary as Mother of God and because she is the Mother of God. This sense of exaltation is strikingly illustrated in a painting by Fra Angelico (fifteenth century) of the coronation of Our Lady. The whole picture is painted in gold; it glows and gleams, and Mary is seated in humble posture before her son who places a crown on her head.

We remember also that in the glorious mysteries of the rosary the coronation follows the Assumption. The two go together and it is helpful to think of the Assumption as Exaltation, as the dazzling 'reward', so to say, of Mary who gave herself totally to her son and to his saving work. This is suggested in the antiphon to the Benedictus: 'Hail, O Queen of all the world, ever-virgin Mary. You bore Christ the Lord, the *Saviour* of all creation.'

The readings suggested by the Lectionary are Isaiah 9:1-6 and

Luke 1:26-38. The first is one of the well-known Messianic prophecies of Isaiah and presumably we are invited to reflect that Mary would be the mother of him who is 'Mighty-God and Prince of Peace'. Likewise we read in Luke that the Son of the Most High, born of Mary, will be given 'the throne of his ancestor David and will rule over the House of Jacob for ever'. The gospel passage, of course, includes Mary's consent: 'Let it be done to me according to your word' which is the expression of her total self-giving to God and his saving work.

Our Lady of the Rosary
Memoria, 7 October

For an understanding of this celebration (which until the time of Pius X was kept on a Sunday) some historical background is necessary. First, we must consider the development of the Hail Mary and then of the liturgical celebration. The use of what was called the Angelical Salutation *as prayer* was not known until the eleventh century in the west. There is an interesting example in a Coptic collection (*Coptic Ostraca*, p. 3) of about the year 600 that runs like this:

> Hail Mary, full of grace, the Lord is with thee, blessed art thou among women, and blessed the fruit of thy womb, because thou didst conceive Christ, the Son of God, the redeemer of souls.

It is interesting because 'Mary' is already introduced into the text (it is of course not in the gospel) and the greeting of Elizabeth is added to the message of the angel. There is also the 'because', a word that echoes the gospel and gives the reason for addressing Mary: she is the mother of the Son of God who is also our Redeemer. There is, however, no petition nor do we know whether it was used in the liturgy or was simply a private prayer.

In the west there was the offertory chant for the fourth Sunday of Advent which is found in the Gregorian Sacramentary (of the eighth century), which begins, 'Ave Maria...' and ends *'ventris tui'*, in other words, the first half of the Hail Mary only. Whether it had any influence on popular devotion is not known. It is not until the eleventh century that we begin to have evidence that the Salutation was being used. Sometimes it was simply 'Ave Maria: Hail Mary, full of grace' to which was soon added 'and blessed is the fruit of thy womb'. Here we have to take account of the Latin text of Luke which in many manuscripts added to the angel's salutation the words of Elizabeth, 'blessed art thou among women'. It was inevitable that the two phrases should be joined. However, in the Little Office of the Blessed Virgin Mary, which at this time was added to the *Divine Office* in monasteries and other religious houses (of canons, cathedral chapters) and had a considerable influence in propagating devotion to our Lady (as she began to be called at this time: in Latin *Domina nostra*), the invitatory of 'mattins' '*Ave Maria, gratia plena*', probably promoted the use of this salutation in a wide variety of circumstances.

The 'second half' of the Hail Mary was slow to develop. There is a prayer as early as the eleventh century for Mary's help at the hour of death; in Dante we find a petition addressed to Mary for pardon, grace and paradise, and in the preaching of St Bernadine of Siena, in the fifteenth century, we find, '*ora pro nobis peccatoribus*' (pray for us sinners). It was not, however, until the sixteenth century that the 'second half' became firmly attached to the Hail Mary: 'Holy Mary, Mother of God, pray for us sinners now and at the hour of our death.'[2]

The use of beads to assist prayer is very old, pre-Christian it seems, and for lay-brothers in monasteries it was offered to them as a substitute for the choir Office in the form of 150 Pater Nosters (Our Fathers) on the pattern of the 150 psalms of the psalter. As it came to be used by other unlettered people, it became known as the 'poor man's psalter'. In the twelfth and early thirteenth century there developed what was called Our Lady's Psalter which consisted of 150 Hail Marys. This was much propagated by a Dominican, Alain de la Roche, in the fifteenth century and he also proposed meditations on the incarnation, the passion and the glorification of Christ to be made on the 150 Hail Marys. By the early sixteenth century, the fifteen Mysteries of the Rosary, as we now know them, were organised and the saying of the Rosary in this form became very popular, as it has remained to this day.[3]

During the battle of Lepanto (1571), the Confraternity of the
Rosary was very active in praying for victory over the Turks,
which in fact turned out to be the case, and in 1573 Pope Gregory
XIII granted a feast of the Holy Rosary for the city of Rome. It
was at this time that the prayer of the Rosary received the final
form we know now: it is divided into tens (decades), each preceded by the Our Father and concluded with the Glory be; five
decades make up the Rosary of fifty invocations to our Lady and
three fifties make up the whole Rosary. It is in this form that the
Rosary has been propagated throughout the church. The Roman
commemoration of 1573 was extended to the whole of the western church in 1716 by Pope Clement XI under the title of the
Feast of the Holy Rosary. The title was more properly changed
to Our Lady of the Rosary in 1960 and this was endorsed by the
Roman Calendar of 1969.

Some special features of the liturgy of the day may be noted. The
first reading of the Mass is Acts 1:12-14 (Mary was at prayer
with the apostles before Pentecost), the psalm may be the
Magnificat in whole or in part, and the gospel is Luke 1:26-30.
The antiphons of the *Divine Office* evoke several of the mysteries
of the Rosary: the annunciation, the birth of Jesus, Mary standing by the cross, when she was made mother of the church, and
her exaltation (i.e. assumption and coronation).

In the Office of Readings, St Bernard invites us to meditate on
the Word of God, the fount of wisdom, who will become flesh
through Mary. But for this, God would have remained unknow-
able; he is above our understanding, he is unapproachable but
through his birth from Mary he can be seen and pondered on.
How, the saint asks? We seen him 'lying in a manger, resting on
the Virgin's bosom, preaching on the mount, spending the night
in prayer; or hanging on the cross, the pallor of death on his face,
like one foresaken among the dead, over-ruling the powers of
hell; or rising again on the third day, showing the apostles the
print of the nails, the sign of victory, and finally ascending from
their sight into heaven.' Thus we are called to meditate on the
joyful, sorrowful and glorious mysteries of the Rosary.

The historical note placed before the Office has a statement that neatly sums up the sense of the celebration: (It) urges all 'to meditate on the mysteries of Christ, following the example of the Blessed Virgin Mary who was in a special manner associated with the incarnation, passion and glorious resurrection of the Son of God'.

Our Lady of Guadalupe
Feast (in USA), 12 December

On 9 December 1531 Juan Diego, a poor Indian, forty-five years old and a Christian for seven years, was hurrying over a hill called Tepeyac on his way to Mexico City for religious instruction. While still on the hill, he heard music in the air and a Lady appeared to him. She told him to go to the local bishop to give him a message that she wanted him to build a chapel on the spot. The bishop was naturally reluctant to do so. Juan went back to the Lady and informed her of this. She told him to come again the next day and also said, 'Do not be afraid, you have nothing to fear. Am I not your compassionate mother?' But Juan did not do so. He had a sick uncle and had to go and find a priest to minister to him. On 12 December he returned and she told him to go to the top of the hill and gather some roses which, in spite of the season, he found fresh and in blossom and the Lady told him to go to the bishop. He gathered the roses in his cloak, went to the bishop, the roses fell out before an astonished bishop and an image of the Lady appeared on the cloak. The bishop was convinced of the truth of Juan's statements and by 1533 the first shrine or sanctuary of Our Lady of Guadalupe was built.[4]

The appearances are well attested though there are slight differences in the accounts that have come down to us. What is consistent in all accounts is the appearance of the Lady, the vision or experience of Juan Diego, the image and the acceptance by the bishop of Juan's story. The differences can be explained by the facts that Juan knew no Spanish and the bishop did not know Juan's language. A protégé of his, one González, acted as an interpreter and seems to have done his job faithfully. One variant in the accounts should perhaps be noted. According to this, the roses fell out of Juan's cloak 'and beneath them the painted image of the Lady'.[5] The first account, as given above, seems to be the one favoured by the authorities who write on this matter.

The image of our Lady is not without its interest and import-
ance. The dress is described as 'European' by which I suppose is
meant Spanish, her face appears to be like that of the people
(*Mestizos*) whom the Spaniards had brutally repressed, and the
decorations on the cloak are those of the local art. Again we are
lost for an explanation but it clear that the image has a symbolic
significance. Juan Diego may well have seen images of our Lady
of Spanish provenance but as a man of fifty he would have been
well aware of the native Aztec art. Here was the beginning of a
new culture (or more exactly, an example of inculturation) in
which, however, for centuries the Spanish had the upper hand,
and the sufferings of the people, the Amerindians, were remembered. As we have seen, the Lady revealed herself as the
Compassionate Mother, the Mother of an afflicted people, or in
another terminology, Our Lady of Consolation. This, we may
suppose, is one reason why devotion to Our Lady has never
ceased throughout the centuries and has spread throughout the
Americas and beyond. In more recent decades so great and so
numerous have been the pilgrims that a vast new basilica has
been built which can accommodate 20,000 people and is described as a church of great beauty.

Synodal, episcopal and papal approval of the shrine of Our
Lady of Guadalupe has not been wanting. In 1737 she was declared patroness of the city of Mexico and a little later of the
whole of 'new Spain'. Pius X (1910) named her Patroness of
Latin America and Pius XII in 1945 called her the 'Queen of
Mexico and Empress of the Americas'. In 1754 Benedict XIV
granted a Mass and Office for the feast kept on 12 December.

The commemoration of Our Lady of Guadalupe is a feast in the
United States and the liturgy of the day is taken from the
Common of the Blessed Virgin Mary with proper prayers for the
occasion. The Opening Prayer recalls the appearance of the
Virgin Mary at Guadalupe and the assembly is invited, with the
help of Mary's prayers, to accept each other as brothers and sisters.
Through justice thus present in the hearts of all 'may peace reign
in the world'.

In the Prayer after Communion the assembly prays that through
the reception of the Body and Blood of Christ they may be 'rec-

onciled' in his love and 'May we who rejoice in the Holy Mother of Guadalupe live united and at peace in this world'. The emphasis on love, justice, reconciliation and peace is clear and reflects the concerns of those who will use these prayers.

It is pleasant to know that Juan Diego, now Blessed, is not forgotten. He is remembered on 9 December with a Mass for Holy Men. The prayer for the day recalls the appearance of Our Lady whom Juan made known to the people and goes on to ask that we may do the will of God following the example and 'counsel' of Mary our Mother.

Notes

1. See Donald Attwater, *The Penguin Dictionary Of Saints* (Harmonsworth, 1963), 'Bernadette', pp. 68-9.

2. For all the forgoing see Herbert Thurston, SJ, *Familiar Prayers. Their Origin and History.* Selected and arranged by Paul Grosjean, SJ, (London, 1953), pp. 90-114.

3. See *A New Dictionary of Liturgy and Worship.* Ed. J. G. Davies (SCM Press, 1986), s.v. 'Rosary' (C. J. Walsh), pp. 471-2.

4. I have followed the account of P. Wallace Platt, CSB, in *Clergy Review*, March, 1978, Vol. LXIII, No 3, pp 109-112.

5. See *New Catholic Encyclopedia*, Vol VI, (McGraw-Hill), 1967, s.v. Guadalupe, Our Lady of, pp 821-822. See also *Encyclopedia of Catholicism*, Ed. R.P. O'Brien (Harper/Collins, 1995), pp 594-596.

CHAPTER 14

Some Marian Chants and Prayers

Devotion to Mary has taken many forms over the centuries. In the eastern parts of the church there were (and are) many kinds of chants but above all the *Akathistos* Hymn of which a brief account is given below. In the west, devotion to Mary developed more slowly until the early eleventh century when chants, hymns, sermons and liturgical texts and non-liturgical texts began to proliferate. The two well known antiphons (or anthems), *Alma Redemptoris Mater* and *Salve Regina* are of this period, the second the most popular to this day. They *became* liturgical texts and were at first sung after compline, often in procession to an image of our Lady. With two others to be considered below, they were ordered to be sung after Lauds (Morning Prayer) and Vespers (Evening Prayer) by Pope Pius V in the revision of the *Divine Office* in 1568. They were to be sung in this order: The *Alma Redemptoris* from Advent to 2 February; the *Ave Regina caelorum* from that date until the end of Lent (exclusive of the last three days of Holy Week); the *Regina caeli* from Easter Sunday until Pentecost; the *Salve Regina* for the rest of the year. In the Cistercian and Dominican rites it was sung throughout the year. In the reform of the *Divine Office* following the Second Vatican Council, apart from the *Regina caeli*, the other three may be sung at any time during the year. To these have been added a number of optional chants. By current regulations they are obligatory only after compline but there would seem to be no reason why one of them should not be sung after Evening Prayer, especially when there is a congregation. A procession, as often in the Middle Ages, could be made to the Lady Chapel or the shrine of our Lady.

A few notes on these four anthems (here thus named for that is what they are used as now) follow.

Alma Redemptoris Mater

I borrow from the Westminster Hymnal (1940) a fairly free translation (no. 261a).

> Mother of Christ! hear thou thy people's cry,
> Star of the deep, and portal of the sky!
> Mother of him who thee from nothing made,
> Sinking we strive, and call to thee for aid:
> Oh, by that joy which Gabriel brought to thee,
> Thou Virgin first and last, let us thy mercy see.

The first line omits *Alma*, an affectionate term, which can be translated 'dear' or 'loving', the latter perhaps being preferable. Borrowing, it seems, from the *Ave, maris stella* we have 'star of the deep'. The phrase 'portal of the sky' conceals the sense. The Latin word is *caeli* ('heaven', not 'sky') and the phrase means that Mary was the one through whom Jesus came into this world and she is also the 'door' through which we may approach God. It is an ancient theme found as early as Irenaeus (+ c. 200), at least as to the first part. The text continues: we are a fallen people and we ask for Mary's aid. In the Latin there is a play on the words *Eva* and *Ave*, again an ancient theme: Mary is seen as reversing the disobedience of Eva. But it is difficult to turn into English without some rather precious gymnastics. Mary is ever-virgin (*prius and posterius*), before and after the birth of Jesus. To conclude we pray that she will have 'mercy' on us, and if that word seems too strong for some, we can quite legitimately translate it 'pity'. These few comments do not do justice to the poetry of the anthem as it is in Latin, but they may help those who wish to sing it in Latin, either in the solemn plainsong which is very moving, or in the famous setting by Palestrina. The anthem has been attributed to Herman the Cripple (*Contractus*) who died in 1054 but there is insufficient evidence for this. It is, however, perhaps the earliest of the Marian anthems.

Ave, Regina Caelorum

This short but lyrical anthem was in fact used as an antiphon at the Office of None on the feast of the Assumption of the Blessed Virgin Mary. Its author is unknown but it was in use in the twelfth century. In the Westminster Hymnal it is translated as follows (no. 262a):

> Hail, O Queen of heaven enthroned!
> Hail, by angels mistress owned,
> Root of Jesse! Gate of morn!
> Whence the world's true light was born:
> Glorious Virgin, joy to thee,
> Loveliest whom in heaven they see.
> Fairest thou where all are fair!
> Plead with Christ our sins to spare.

Little commentary is necessary. Mary is Queen of heaven and of the angelic host, yet her origin is earthly. According to the tradition she was of the house of David, whose father was Jesse. She is 'gate of morn' for she brought forth 'the world's true light', the Saviour of the world. In the Latin the anthem ends '*pro nobis Christum exora*'; the translator has expanded this for the sake of his metre but, following the Latin, we can be sure that Mary prays for us in a variety of our needs.

Regina caeli (W. H. 263)

Somewhere towards the end of the twelfth century or the beginning of the thirteenth, this was used as an antiphon in the Office of Easter time. It was propagated by the Franciscans and was inserted into the *Divine Office* as the Easter anthem in the fourteenth century, presumably with its many alleluias. Shorn of those alleluias, it is very brief indeed and it comes alive only when it is sung in the solemn tone.

> Joy to thee, O Queen of Heaven! alleluia.
> He whom thou wast meet to bear; alleluia.
> As he promised (he) hath risen; alleluia.
> Pour for us to him thy prayer; alleluia.

(I have changed the fourth line which is without a subject: 'as promised hath arisen', which will not do).

The meaning is clear; all one would do is to point to the 'meet to bear' phrase. This translates the Latin '*meruisti*' which in Christian Latin has not the force of 'deserving'. It was by the grace of the Holy Spirit that Mary was *enabled* to bring forth the Son of God.

Salve Regina

Hail holy Queen, mother of mercy;
hail our life, our sweetness and our hope.
To thee do we cry, poor banished children of Eve;
to thee do we send up our sighs, mourning and weeping
in this vale of tears.
Turn, then, most gracious advocate, thine eyes of mercy
towards us;
and after this our exile, show unto us the blessed fruit of
thy womb, Jesus.
O clement, O loving, O sweet Virgin Mary.

(This translation has been the best known and popular translation current for a very long time in the Catholic community in
England).

Various authors have been suggested at one time or another for
this anthem but none of the attributions can be supported with
any security. It is certain that it was not composed by St Bernard
(it pre-existed him) and there is insufficient evidence to support
the authorship of Adhémar, Bishop of Le Puy. All we can say is
that it was known in the later decades of the eleventh century
and that probably the author of the anthem wrote both words
and chant. This latter in the solemn tone (evidently traditional as
there are variations in the musical texts of the Benedictine,
Cistercian and Roman books) is very moving. Sung in the fading
evening light in a monastic church before an image of Our Lady,
it touches deep chords in the heart. The simple tone, the one
most people know, is less impressive and its date is unknown to
this writer.

The Christian is looking to the pitiful Mary, who is Queen, and
seeks her help. It seems that the word 'Mater' (mother) was not
in the earliest texts but it certainly makes the first line run more
easily. In the second line the Carthusian texts had 'dulcedo vitae'
(sweetness of our life) for 'vita, dulcedo', an obvious attempt to
soften the meaning; in what sense is Mary our 'life'? It is difficult
to say and so the Carthusians made it more comprehensible:
Mary, as we contemplate her, is our 'sweetness', our joy, our

pleasure. It is, however, a change that seems to be unsupported by other texts.

The cries of the Christians are urgent: '*Ad te clamamus ... ad te suspiramus...*; we are aware that here we have no abiding city (Heb 13:14). As long as we are in this world we are in a valley of tears (Ps 83:7) So we beseech the Queen of mercy, the advocate, the one who pleads for us, and we ask her to turn her gentle and pitiful eyes towards us and to hold out to us Jesus, the blessed fruit of her womb. The prayer ends in a sigh: 'O gentle, O loving, O kind Mary'. (The word 'virgin' is apparently an addition).[1]

Stabat Mater

This hymn, once very popular, was written as a poem in the late thirteenth century and is certainly of Franciscan inspiration. Its authorship is usually attributed to Jacopone da Todi (in Umbria) but now it seems scholarly opinion is in favour of St Bonaventure. When, in the early eighteenth century, the feast of the Seven Sorrows of the Blessed Virgin Mary was inserted into the Roman Calendar, this hymn was appointed as a Sequence in the Mass (sung after the epistle) and in sections for the Hours of the *Divine Office*. It is now optional for the Mass.

At one time it was used devotionally for the Stations of the Cross, a stanza being sung after each station. With the decline of that devotion, there has been a decline in the popularity of the hymn and perhaps many Catholics do not know it at all. There have been several translations into English, the best known begins 'At the cross her station keeping'. There is another in the *Westminster Hymnal*, no. 37, by the late Mgr R. A. Knox.

Ave maris stella

This lyrical hymn has the distinction of being, in all probability, the earliest Marian hymn of the Latin church. It seems to have been written in the ninth century and it has retained its popularity ever since. The epithet '*maris stella*' or '*stella maris*' has appealed to many who go down to the sea in ships. It seems to have been first found in this hymn. There have been many translations and that by Fr E. Caswall (+1878) has much to be said for it. The first verse runs as follows:

Hail, thou star of ocean,
Portal of the sky;
Ever Virgin Mother
of the Lord most high.
Oh! By Gabriel's *Ave*,
uttered long ago, Eve's name reversing,
'Stablish peace below.

It is clear that here we have traditional themes: Mary is the Gate of Heaven, through whom the Saviour came into this world and she prays for us that we may go to heaven. There is the usual play on Ave and Eva: the obedience of Mary cancels out the disobedience of Eve.

The fourth stanza is a very compact and elegant piece of Latin:

Monstra te esse Matrem,
Sumat per te preces
Qui pro nobis natus
Tulit esse tuus.

Turned as follows by Fr Caswall:
Show thyself a mother:
offer him our sighs (prayers)
who for us incarnate
did not thee despise.

This last line is perhaps not so happy: the Latin has it that the Son of God responded to the consent of Mary as he in return consented to be born of her. R. A. Knox in this respect is better: 'Offer Christ our praying – still thy word obeying – whom on earth thou barest.' (See *W. H.* no. 101). The whole hymn, brief though it is, is very prayerful.

There are of course many other Marian hymns but not so many fresh compositions, outside the range of the liturgical hymns, that are good. The shortage of really good vernacular hymns is rather surprising.

Sub tuum praesidium

This prayer does not seem to be as well known as it once was so
I append the Latin text and a translation.

> *Sub tuum praesidium confugimus,*
> *Sancta Dei Genetrix,*
> *nostras deprecationes ne despicias in necessitatibus,*
> *sed a periculis cunctis libera nos semper,*
> *Virgo gloriosa et benedicta.*

> Holy Mother of God,
> we seek your help and protection.
> Look kindly on us as we pray to you in our needs;
> deliver us from every danger that threatens us.
> Be with us always, O blessed and glorious Virgin.

During the last hundred years or so thousands of papyri have
been discovered, mostly in Egypt. Among them was one, now
preserved in the John Rylands Library in Manchester, on which
is written the above prayer in Greek. Scholarly opinion as to its
date ranged from possibly fourth or even fifth century to the
third century, but now it seems to be agreed that it is of the third
century, perhaps about 250 AD. One reason for the difference of
opinion was the presence in it of the word *Theotokos*, translated
in the Latin as *Dei Genetrix*. But the appellation *Theotokos* (with
all its implications) was defined as of faith only at the Council of
Ephesus in 431. It was, however, in use before that date. It was
current in the church of Alexandria in the fourth century and it
occurs in sermon by Proclus, the Patriarch of Constantinople, in
428/9 (see for example *Divine Office*, III, p. 526, for part translation) and was already traditional. Much earlier, in the middle of
the third century, it was used by the Christian writer Origen
who died in 254. There can be little doubt that this is the oldest
prayer *to* Mary, and to her as *Theotokos*, the God-bearer, or as the
Latin has it, Mother of God.

The experts tell us that the original Greek is rhythmical and, as
can be seen, the prayer is in the first person plural. This indicates
that it was not simply a private prayer but that of a community.
It seems then to have been what we would call a liturgical

prayer. The last phrase, *Virgo gloriosa et benedicta*, is an addition made by the Latin translator. In the Latin church it has often been used as an antiphon to the Litany of Loreto and may now be used after Compline. The sense of the prayer is very clear. Addressing Mary as *Theotokos*, we seek her protection and help. Whatever our needs or whatever the dangers we may be in, there is the sense that she will be with us. In short, it is a confident prayer asking for her intercession and support.

The Akathistos Hymn

The Greek *Akathistos* Hymn is perhaps the finest hymn to the Blessed Virgin Mary in the Christian church. Its composition is attributed to St Romanos Meldós (+ c. 560) but it contains texts of the eighth century referring to the defeat of the Muslims in 717-18. It is sung in part in the Greek Orthodox Church during Small Compline on the first five Fridays of Lent, the whole being recited on the fifth Friday. In the Russian Orthodox Church it is sung in whole on the Saturday of the fifth week of Lent at Matins. It is quite long, covering just over nine pages in the English translation. It must also be something of a test of endurance as it is sung standing throughout (hence its name). Its literary form is a little complicated. It is made up of long stanzas (*ikoi*) and shorter ones (*kontakia*) and these latter have a certain narrative element. They are based on the infancy gospels from the annunciation to the presentation of Jesus in the temple. The long stanzas are salutations or greetings to Mary, thirteen in number, that begin 'Hail' (*Chaire*, 'Rejoice') and end 'Hail, Bride without bridegroom'. Mary is both Virgin and Mother. As in one greeting or acclamation she is hailed the 'womb of the divine incarnation', and because she bears the Son of God, she is the 'throne of God'. In Kontakion 2 the divine conception is recalled: the power of the Most High overshadows her and he makes her 'a fruitful womb and a fertile field' and the harvest is salvation. The mystery of the incarnation is proclaimed and pondered on (and perhaps we take it too much for granted) and Mary is seen in the context of salvation history: she is the heavenly ladder by which Christ comes down to us. She is the 'gate of the hallowed mystery' and the bridge leading us from earth to heaven. She foreshadows the glory of the resurrection (we are meant to understand that the body she bore was the body that rose again to glory). She is the 'enclosure of God' containing him whom nothing can enclose, a phrase recalling the western phrase that comes from the Old Testament: Mary is the *hortus conclusus*, the enclosed garden whence comes the Son of God. She also prefigures the baptismal font for she bears within her the source of grace, Jesus Christ.

Many other acclamations hymn the glory of Mary and among them we find terms that are familiar in the west. Mary is 'gate' (*Ianua caeli*), she is tabernacle of God the Word, she is Ark 'made golden by the Spirit', she is mother of the Star, that is Christ, the Daystar or Sun that rises in the east; she is the 'bridal chamber' (cf. Ps 18) for she joins the faithful to their Lord. She is star herself for she brings forth the Sun of Justice.

This and much else is to be found in the Akathistos Hymn for which see *The Akathistos Hymn to the Most Holy Mother of God*, published by the Ecumenical Society of the Blessed Virgin Mary (1987), translations by Mother Mary, Bishop Kallistos and Roger Green.

Notes

1. For the history of the *Salve Regina* and the *Regina caeli* see H. Thurston, SJ, *Familiar Prayers* (1953) pp. 118-145 and pp. 146-151. For the *Alma Redemptoris* and the *Ave Regina caelorum* and other liturgical hymns here referred to see Joseph Connelly, *Hymns of the Roman Liturgy* (1957), pp. 44-47, pp. 186-190 (*Stabat Mater*).

CHAPTER 15

The Psalms in the Marian Feasts

The use of the psalms in the Marian feasts is based on their Christian interpretation which has a long history going back to the New Testament itself. In the Acts of the Apostles alone we find a number of psalms that are seen as referring to Christ: for example: Acts 2:25, 28, 30/ Psalm 15; Psalm 109; Acts 4:11/Psalm 117; Acts 4:25/Psalm 2. In Hebrews 1:8, 9 there is a quotation from Psalm 44. In the Christian tradition this was accepted, and the continued use of the psalms was seen as justified by this interpretation. The next step was to find texts that were applicable to Mary, the mother of Christ. It is a matter of some delicacy as we cannot expect to find direct references to Mary in the psalter. In fact, to find a key to what is called the 'accommodated sense' we have to go to other places in the Bible. One of the themes of the prophets (as in some other places of the Old Testament) is Israel as the bride of God (cf. Hos, 1 and 2). Then the vision concentrates on Zion-Jerusalem as standing for the whole people of God. Thus in the context of the restoration of Israel we have the outburst of Zephaniah (3:14, 15):

> Sing aloud, O daughter of Zion,
> Shout, O Israel!
> Rejoice and exult with all your heart,
> O daughter of Jerusalem!
> The king of Israel is *in your midst*.

There is a similar text in Zechariah (9:9):

> Rejoice heart and soul, daughter of Zion!
> Shout with gladness, daughter of Jerusalem!
> See how your king comes to you, victorious....

Both these readings are appointed for the day hours of the Solemnity of Mary, 1 January. Both are regarded as Messianic texts and so applicable to Mary, the Mother of the Messiah. She is 'the daughter of Zion', 'the daughter of Jerusalem'; she is the place of the Temple, the Holy City where God dwells. So we have intimations of a liturgical use of these texts in the Marian offices. With texts of Isaiah the metaphor changes; Israel is called wife and mother. In chapter 62, Zion, once abandoned, 'forsaken', with the restoration and the return from exile she is the 'wedded', she is now called 'my delight in her', and from her 'salvation is coming', with him (the Messiah) comes 'his reward', his 'achievement preceding him' (verses 10, 11). The text continues:

> They will be called 'The Holy People', 'The Lord's Redeemed', while you will be called 'Sought-after', 'City not forsaken'.

Zion, Jerusalem, will become a fruitful mother. This is made explicit in chapter 66:10-13:

> Rejoice with Jerusalem, be glad for her, you who love her!
> Rejoice, rejoice with her, all you who mourned her!
> …
> You will be suckled, carried on her hip
> and fondled in her lap.
> As a mother comforts a child
> so shall I comfort you;
> you will be comforted in Jerusalem.

To these texts must be added some others from the New Testament. Obviously the first one to turn to is Revelation 21:2-4. There is the holy city, the new Jerusalem 'as beautiful as a bride all dressed for her husband'. Then the voice comes from heaven proclaiming, 'You see this city? Here God lives among men. He will make his home among them; they shall be his people, and he will be their God; his name is God-with-them' (cf. Ezek 37:37 and Isa 7:14). This clearly takes up the imagery of the Old Testament concerning the people of God being 'married' to Yahweh in a covenant of love, the everlasting love of Jeremiah 31:3, which will be continued in the New Testament because God's love is ever faithful.

This notion is found in Ephesians 5:1, 2 which begins with the statement about the sacrificial love of Christ for his people and, later in the same chapter, continues with the church as the sacrament-symbol of the union of Christ with his people: 'This mystery (sacramentum) is great', profound, says the writer, and it refers first of all to the church. It is of this mystery that human marriage is a reflection, a sign, itself in turn a sacrament, illuminating in its real though limited way the union between Christ and his church.

From all this we can deduce that the Bible in different but related texts sees the people of God as at once the spouse of the Most High and as the mother of those who are to become a restored people (cf. Isa 66). Jerusalem, the holy city, first in the Old Testament and then the restored Jerusalem in the New Testament (not yet fully realised), stands for the whole people of God. It is in this sense that the Jerusalem-Zion of the psalms was applied to the church, the new people of God. Since the Jesus Mary bore in her womb was the life-giving head of the new people of God, she has a special relationship with them. She is the mother of Jesus Christ and through him she is the mother of those who are 'born of him through water and the Holy Spirit'.

To understand this way of thinking we need to see how in their reflections on the psalms the Fathers of the church found a reference to this matter. The key psalm is one that seems an unlikely text to begin with. Psalm 18 (19) is a hymn of praise to God the creator of all things: 'The heavens proclaim the glory of God, and the firmament shows forth the work of his hands.' Then we see a specification of the works of his hands: he places a tent for the sun; and it comes forth like a bridegroom coming from its tent and runs its course from one end of the sky to the other like a champion. In the Latin (which is based on the Greek translation) 'tent' is translated 'thalamus' which means bedroom or, more specifically, the marriage bed. Quite early too the 'champion' was seen as Christos-Helios, Christ the Sun of Justice or righteousness. From these images, the Fathers constructed the sense that this psalm was a celebration of the incarnation. The Son of God is conceived in the womb of Mary, taking from her our human nature and through it the whole of humanity. There was

at this point a 'marriage' between the Son of God and those people who would be made and called his own through baptism.
These are the Christian church and of this church Mary is the
model, the image and the exemplar. As some of the Fathers said,
the church came to birth in her womb, she is the first church,
until the followers of her son would be incorporated into the
body of which he is the head.

Two writers, one from the east and one from the west, show
how these notions developed. The first is Sophronius, Patriarch
of Jerusalem (+638), from a sermon of whom the following is extracted:

> She who gave birth to God enclosed within her womb him
> who lives in you according to the flesh and he comes forth
> from you like a bridegroom, giving joy to all and sharing his
> divine light with all mankind. In you, O Virgin, as in the clear
> brightness of heaven, God 'has placed his tent' and he will
> come forth from you like a bridegroom from his chamber.
> Like a giant he will run the course of his life to bring salva-
> tion to all living things (*Divine Office*, III, p. 512).

Here are what one might call the christological nuptials; here is
motherhood and here is the message of salvation through Christ
who is at once the son and the bridegroom of Mary and so later
of the church, the whole people of God. In the second text, which
comes from the Cistercian abbot Guerric of the twelfth century,
it is motherhood that is stressed:

> Mary bore only one son. In heaven, he is the only-begotten of
> the Father; on earth likewise, he is the only-begotten of his
> mother. She who is the only Virgin-Mother, she who glories
> in having borne the only-begotten of the Father, embraces
> that only-begotten of hers in *all his members* so that she can be
> truly called mother of all in whom she sees that Christ has
> been formed or is being formed (*D.V.* III, p. 527; italics
> mine).[1]

There is then here a multiplicity of images, Bride/Bridegroom,
Virginal-Mother and mother of all those reborn in Christ her
son. There may even seem to be a conflict of images, but where

the event is unique we must expect to find many images of a series of unique events. For the accommodated sense of the psalms the situation is clearer. From the images of the church as mother, Christians came to see that it could be applied to Mary herself as the first church and as the mother of baptised Christians in the sense given above. The bridal image, however, must be treated with great caution. Mary does not *beget* the children of God and the scriptures, and the fathers after them, are very careful never to suggest anything remotely resembling such a notion. It is the *church* that is the bride of Christ and it is he who, communicating his life to them through word and sacrament, brings into existence children who are children of the Father and children of the church. As Virgin-Mother, however she is the one in whom the Son of God dwelt and lived and this we find emphasised in the psalms that are appointed to be sung in the liturgy.

We can now turn to the psalms that are used on the feasts of the Blessed Virgin Mary. Psalm 18:2-7 is used less often than might have been expected. It occurs in the Office of Readings for Christmas Day where it is seen as a reference to the incarnation. The sun, now turned into a person, is the bridegroom coming forth from his tent, in the Latin the *thalamus*, celebrating the 'marriage' between Mary as the church and Jesus Christ who is its bridegroom. He is beginning his course that will reach to the ends of the earth. His birth is salvific, he is beginning his work of salvation that will reach out to the whole human race. Incarnation and soteriology were not separated in the early centuries of the church as they were in the manuals of theology in more recent times.

Likewise, Psalm 44 is used only sparingly, perhaps because it is regarded primarily as a Messianic psalm. Yet verses 11-18 are very appropriate to feasts of Our Lady. The psalm is a wedding song. The king is the great warrior who yet loves truth, goodness and right. He is anointed by Yahweh 'above other kings' (cf. Heb 1:9) and is now awaiting his bride in his 'ivory place'. She appears in all her beauty and is bidden to forget her own people so that she may be united in marriage with the king. She for her part is 'clothed with splendour, her robes (are) embroid-

ered with pearls set in gold.' Thus gloriously robed, she with her
maiden companions enters the royal palace and to her will be
granted 'sons in place of her own people' and her name will be
ever remembered. This last phrase has a curious echo in the
Magnificat: 'all nations will call me blessed'. But once again this
psalm seems, in this accommodated sense, to refer to Mary, as
the symbol of the church and its many peoples. If we wished to
indulge in allegory, we can see in the splendid robes an indication of the grace that Mary received from God so that she could
become the fitting mother of Jesus, the Son of God.

The psalms most often used for almost all the feasts of the
Blessed Virgin Mary are understandably grouped together in
the Common of the B.V.M. For First Vespers (Evening Prayer)
there is Psalm 112, 'Praise, servants of the Lord, praise the name
of the Lord'. As a Marian psalm it does not look very promising
until we read that the Lord God looks down from his throne on
the lowly, which reminds us of the lowly handmaid of the
Magnificat and of her rejoicing in the Lord who has done great
things for her. There is what seems to be intended as a more direct reference to Mary in the last verse: 'To the childless wife he
gives a home/ and gladdens her heart with children'; this is underlined in its own way by the antiphon: 'Blessed are you,
Virgin Mary: you carried the Creator of all things'.

This is followed by another psalm of praise, 'O praise the Lord,
Jerusalem' (147). We note the word 'Jerusalem' used here of
Mary as the mother and figure of the church. But a note in the
New Jerusalem Bible (g, p. 1506) suggests another view: 'The
word of God (mentioned in the psalm) is represented here as a
messenger, almost as a person.' It seems then that verse 15, 'He
sends his word to the earth', is a somewhat obscure reference to
the annunciation in Luke 1:28-35. The word of God has power, it
penetrates Mary's being and brings about the conception of the
Saviour. But we note also verse 13, 'He has blessed children
within you'.

There are three psalms for the Office of Readings, 23, 45, 86, of
which the first was once appointed for the feast of Christmas. It
is about one who is approaching the holy place, Zion, where is

the temple of the Lord. Such a one ('he' in the original) is pure of heart and will receive blessings from Yahweh, the Lord. This seems to be accommodated to Mary. The second part of the psalm (7-10) however is applied to Christ. Who is it that is approaching the gates of the holy place? 'He is king of glory', the Lord Jesus Christ who is called *Kyrios* (Lord) in the New Testament. We are, I think, invited to see Mary as 'the holy place', Zion; the Lord Jesus is coming to her to dwell with her and in the fulness of time to come forth from her at that time we now call Christmas. If this seems too far-fetched, we can think simply of Jesus, the Lord of glory, being born of Mary.

Psalm 45 again is about the holy place, God's city, to which the waters flowing round it bring joy. The text continues, 'God is within' it and he will continue to be with it 'at the dawning of the day'. This psalm has been applied to Mary for a very long time and it was all the easier to do so as in the Latin, the 'city' was *civitas*, a feminine noun. God is with Mary and he will be with her forever. But like Psalm 86, which is to follow, the primary emphasis seems to be on Mary as the image of the church and the application to her comes from that.

Psalm 86 may be seen as the classical psalm expressing the symbolism Zion-Church-Mary. It speaks of the holy mountain, Zion, as the 'city of God' of which are told glorious things. People from all parts of the earth will acknowledge her and will become her children, people from Babylon, Egypt, Philistia, Tyre, Ethiopia, and she will be called mother of them all; at the word of the Lord Most High, 'These are her children and in her all will find a home'. Zion, the place of the Temple, was the rallying point of the people of Israel to which they went, singing songs of joy (Ps. 121). In the New Testament it becomes the church into which the new people of God are incorporated by faith, baptism, confirmation and the holy eucharist, and thus become the sons and daughters of God and brothers and sisters of Christ (Rom 8:14, 15, 21, 29). Through their relation with him, they become also children of Mary who bore in her womb and brought forth the Saviour of the human race. It is on this that are built other relations with Mary, relations of affection, devotion, trust, and recourse to her in times of need.

All this may well seem a somewhat complicated way of inter-preting the psalm used in the Marian liturgy but it is important to establish that the filial relationship with Mary is through her son. It is from him that all grace comes and it is that same grace that makes us sons and daughters of God.

In conclusion, it can be said that this way of using the psalms for the Marian liturgy is common to the church of the east and the west. In the Byzantine rite, for instance, on the feast of the Dormition of our Most Holy Lady, Psalms 44 and 131 (both in part) are used and Psalm 23 is referred to (See *The Festal Menaion*, trans. by Mother Mary and Archbishop Kallistos Ware (London, 1969), pp. 504, 509, 510, etc). This is an important witness as the Marian use of the psalms in the eastern churches predates the same use in the west.

Note

1. A very clear statement of the mother-church notion is to be found in a writing of Pacian (4th century), Bishop of Barcelona, on Baptism (PL 13:1092-3 and *D.V.* III, p. 421):

> Christ took a soul and body in the womb of Mary. It is this flesh he came to save… he joined it to his own spirit, making it his own. This is the marriage of the Lord, joined to the flesh of man – a great mys-tery (*sacramentum*) uniting the two – Christ and the church in one flesh. This union is effected by the Holy Spirit who gives birth to the people of God.